T0063063

A Simple Model
of
Biblical Cosmology

F. Carlyle Stebner

WESTBOW
PRESS
A DIVISION OF THOMAS NELSON
& ZONDERVAN

Scripture taken from the Holy Bible, NEW INTERNATIONAL VERSION®. Copyright © 1973, 1978, 1984 by Biblica, Inc. All rights reserved worldwide. Used by permission. NEW INTERNATIONAL VERSION® and NIV® are registered trademarks of Biblica, Inc. Use of either trademark for the offering of goods or services requires the prior written consent of Biblica US, Inc. Information from FoodPhotoSite.com

WestBow Press books may be ordered through booksellers or by contacting:

WestBow Press
A Division of Thomas Nelson & Zondervan
1663 Liberty Drive
Bloomington, IN 47403
www.westbowpress.com
1 (866) 928-1240

ISBN: 978-1-4908-4856-3 (sc)
ISBN: 978-1-4908-4857-0 (e)

Library of Congress Control Number: 2014916752

Printed in the United States of America.

WestBow Press rev. date: 10/06/2014

Contents

Acknowledgments

Unless otherwise noted, Scripture passages are taken from the Holy Bible, New International Version, © 1973, 1978, 1984 by the International Bible Society. Used by permission of Zondervan. All rights reserved.

Scripture quotations marked "ESV" are from the Holy Bible, English Standard Version, © 2001, 2007 by Crossway Bibles, a division of Good News Publishers. Used by permission. All rights reserved.

Job 28 (KJV). "Blue Letter Bible." http://www.blueletterbible.org/Bible.cfm?b=Job&c=28&p=0&rl=0&ss=0&t=KJV

The formulas, calculations, and graphs were obtained using the following resources:

Maplesoft ©2013 Maplesoft, a division of Waterloo Maple, Inc., 615 Kumpf Drive, Waterloo, ON, Canada, N2V1K8. Maplesoft™ Waterloo Maple Inc. The use of this program is noted in the appropriate location by "Maplesoft."

"Off with their heads!"
The Queen of Hearts, *Alice's Adventures in Wonderland*,
Lewis Carroll

Introduction

Many scientists have rejected the Bible and its teachings using the reasoning that all processes must be conjured by the natural laws. Any deviation from this approach is considered unscientific, subject to ridicule and discipline from the academic community. What follow are often censure, dismissal from academic positions, and the inability to publish any view that differs from that of the establishment in refereed journals.

However, in this process, what has been rejected is a viewpoint that is different from that of the established scientific community, rather than an unscientific evaluation of data or facts. What has been lost? In the short term, for students and professors alike is the loss of academic freedom, the unfettered suppression of free discussion of thoughts, opinions, and conclusions. The dictatorship of the professor has been established to the point at which the only response academics have to opinions other than their own is "off with their heads!"

I encourage those who can to "think outside the box" and to consider alternative theories and explanations for the natural world, discoveries made by continuing research and study. If we rely on only one theory, we restrict ourselves and become narrow-minded. Especially to students: keep your mind open, think for yourself, and don't be intimidated by those who happen to have Ph.Ds. Do not be brainwashed by professors who believe only in evolution. If you do not explore alternate theories and opposing opinions, your mind may well become rigid, so your opinion will not really be your own. For teachers and professors: allow free discussion of differing points of view; support academic freedom.

The Bible is more than a source of inspiration for alternative theories of origins, of biological development, and the progress of natural phenomena in general. The Bible tells of God's place in the universe, His relationship to humankind, and His desire for fellowship with people. Most important, however, is God's plan to reconcile humankind to Himself. The long-term plan is for eternity, which is infinitely longer than the age of the universe, whether secular or biblical. To recognize the truths in the Bible requires recognizing the eternal truth that God's Son, Jesus Christ, came to earth in the flesh, was crucified, and died for our sins, thereby completing God's plan for us to be in fellowship with Him. The loss that comes with failing to keep an open mind is much greater than academic freedom for those who reject the Bible and its teachings. The loss is fellowship with God and His Son, Jesus Christ.

The main message of the Bible is spiritual, but, as we shall see, the Bible also provides insight into natural processes and phenomena. After all, God created and set into motion all the natural laws, so it should not be surprising that God's book contains truths about nature as well.

It is my fervent prayer that the comments to follow will inspire all to continue their study of creation by reading the Bible. My hope is also that the thoughts contained herein may be a catalyst for further thought and analysis of scientific data from a creation perspective. Finally, my goal is to glorify God and direct our secular scientific friends to Christ. God's blessing on you all.

"For God so loved the world that he gave his one and only Son, that whoever believes in him shall not perish but have eternal life." (John 3:16 NIV)

"Where were you when I laid the earth's foundation?" (Job 38:4 NIV)

CHAPTER 1

Science in the Bible

Historical Examples

The Bible is not a science textbook. One cannot find the chemical formula for para-amino benzoic acid or Maxwell's electromagnetic formulas in integral form in the Bible. However, the Bible does contain references to such things as natural phenomena that are recognized as being scientific in nature.

As we shall see, these references are not extensive and are sometimes cryptic in nature, so they are likely subject to superficial interpretation or totally overlooked, especially on casual reading. Therefore, to the nonscientist they may not carry much meaning or importance. Let us consider two examples that are well established.

The first example is found in Psalm 8:8(NIV), where we read about "the birds of the air, and the fish of the sea, all that swim the paths of the seas." While mariners know the effects of wind, tides, and waves on vessels and sailing, an in-depth systematic study of these effects had not been done during the early days of seafaring. In 1786 Benjamin Franklin published a letter "Containing Sundry Maritime Observations," in which he describes the Gulf of Mexico's current in the section "Sundry circumstances relating to the Gulph Stream."[1]

However, it was a US Navy officer, Matthew Fontaine Maury, who studied the ocean in detail. Having been raised by a religious father, he learned the Psalms well, and Psalm 8:8 inspired his study of the oceans. Using old ships logs, Maury charted ships courses, the winds, the movement of whales, and other data. These studies led to the publication of Wind and Current Chart of the North Atlantic in 1857 and Physical Geography of the Seas and Its Meteorology in 1861. These publications and his other accomplishments earned Maury the nickname "Father of Modern Oceanography." Maury's studies established the existence of the "paths of the sea" referred to in Psalm 8:8. These "paths of the sea" are now called the various ocean currents.[2]

The second example is in the book of Job, where we read, "To make the weight for the winds; and he weigheth the waters by measure" (Job 28:25, KJV), which the English Standard Version translates as "When he gave to the wind its weight and apportioned the waters by measure." This reference, as you may have guessed, refers to atmospheric pressure, which is the weight of the air over a specified area of Earth's surface. The standard air pressure is 1013.25 hectopascals.

Modern Examples

Are there other passages in the Bible that may be correlated to current secular cosmology theories or descriptions? There are some possibilities, but that the Bible does not necessarily support secular concepts because there are significant differences.

Let's begin at the beginning (a novel idea). The Bible tells us, "In the beginning God created the heavens and the earth" (Genesis 1:1 NIV). Of course, this statement differs significantly from the Big Bang theory. Next we read, "And God said 'Let there be light'" (Genesis 1:3 NIV). Light as we know it is electromagnetic energy. We can say, then, that God created energy first—all the energy necessary to create the universe and everything in it. The Bible then tells us that "God saw that the light was good and he separated the light from the darkness" (Genesis 1:3 NIV).

Genesis 1:6–7 (NIV) continues, "And God said 'let there be an expanse between the waters to separate water from water'. So God made the expanse and separated the water under the expanse from the water above it." Elsewhere we read, "But they deliberately forget that long ago by God's word the heavens existed and the earth was formed out of water and by water" (2 Peter 3:5 NIV). Is there evidence of this creation found today? Look up in the sky at the fluffy, white clouds floating around. Turn on your water faucet, and what comes out? We see water all around us. In fact, life on earth would not be possible without water.

We see comets from time to time, which have been described as dirty ice balls. If they are ice, they must be composed of water; if they are dirty, they must have a component of soil or other solid material, such as rock. These can be seen as the remote remnants of the formative process commanded by God. One source of comets that secular scientists describe is the Kuiper Belt. There is also the "Oort cloud," which secular scientists theorize is the origin of long-period comets. The Oort cloud (like the Hills cloud) has been theorized but not yet identified, although it would not be surprising if they were soon discovered.[3] Comets may be considered as part of the water and earth that was left over from the creation of Earth, other planets, and other solid objects in the universe, such as asteroids.

Russ Humphreys has a wonderful theory regarding the separation of waters. The "waters above" can be seen as a spherical shell—most likely ice crystals—that surrounds the universe, with a total mass of more than 8.8×10^{52} kg. We will see this theory again a little later. This water layer would surely be a lot of water left over from creation.

In addition, more "waters" are being discovered by secular science inside the universe. A 2011 article in the *Digital*

Journal by Andrew Moran reports the discovery of a water cloud that contains 140 trillion times the amount of water on the earth. This mass is evidently around a black hole, identified as a quasar.[4] It is likely that more water in the expanses of space will be found, so it seems that these waters above and waters below are exactly what the Bible says.

The Big Bang

The Big Bang Theory of secular science suggests that the universe began with an incredibly hot, incredibly small "singularity" of energy that formed itself out of nothing and then expanded. Scientists explain that "At that time, which we call the big bang, the density of the universe and the curvature of space-time would have been infinite. ... Such a point is an example of what mathematicians call a singularity."[5] After expansion, the time postulated to produce the universe is incredibly long.

The initial descriptions of the Big Bang suggested a tremendous explosion of a "singularity," as noted above, but today cosmologists say that there was no explosion but a rapid "expansion." However, Associate Professor of Geology Dr. Vic DiVenere, in a lecture at Columbia University pointed out that "This is exactly like a giant explosion. All of the bits move outward away from the center of the explosion."[6] Thus, the scenario now is that "After its initial experience, it" (the singularity) "inflated [the Big Bang], expanded and cooled, going from very, very small and very, very hot to the size and temperature of our current universe."[7] The Big Bang Theory also includes the scenario that "Approximately 10^{-37} seconds into the expansion, a phase transition caused a cosmic inflation, during which the universe grew exponentially."[8] Isn't a dense, hot expansion over 10^{-37} seconds called an explosion? The secular cosmology community should stop playing semantics if the Big Bang started from a "singularity."

An additional aspect of the secular description of the universe is that there is no center to the universe, but if the universe started as a singularity, then the location of the singularity, assuming a spherical expansion, *is* the center of the universe. Thus, secular science would have you believe that the universe started at a point called a singularity, but there is no center of the universe. These are two opposing statements. Is there a center or not? Thus, another secular cosmological oxymoron emerges.

Of course, the secular cosmology community doesn't recognise a center to the universe. Secular science applies the Copernican Principle to the universe as a whole. Copernicus postulated that the sun was the center of the solar system, as opposed to the Ptolemaic universe, where Earth was the center. However, the secular scientist has overextended the theory of Copernicus by applying the principle to the entire universe.

Another aspect of the Big Bang is the theory that the early universe was opaque or "foggy." During a process called "recombination," the universe changed from opaque to transparent. The time required for this process that secularists postulate is significantly longer (378,000 years) than the biblical account,[9] but since God created the energy necessary to form the universe, He could certainly cause a recombination to occur in twenty-four hours. In any case, the secular inflationary epoch is considerably different from that of the biblical model.

One possible reason that secular cosmologists reject a center to the universe is that the concept has spiritual implications. Secular science has avoided the implication that God, as the Creator of humankind as His central creation, places mankind at the center of the universe, and therefore by extension the Earth (or the Milky Way). As suggested by DiVenere above, the Big Bang requires a center; and so if there is a center the theory falls apart on one of its base postulates. However, the model of biblical cosmology postulates a center, and there is observational evidence for this concept.

Consider the observational evidence. Using red shift (z) data, which William Tifft previously processed into "power spectra," and noticing groupings of data around specific z values, creation cosmologist Russell Humphreys[10] showed that the z value data groupings correspond to specific distances. This finding means that there are concentric shells of galaxies distributed at specific distances around the Milky Way. In addition, these groupings could not have occurred by accident. Humphreys demonstrated mathematically that "the probability of our galaxy being so close to the center of the cosmos by accident is less than 1 in 1 trillion," so we have observational and mathematical evidence of our galaxy being close to the center of the universe.

Consider some examples of observations from earth logically. Figure 1 shows that the distribution of galaxies around the Milky Way is similar in all directions, even though these galaxies are not homogeneous. If our observations show galaxies in all directions, doesn't this suggest a central location for the Milky Way?

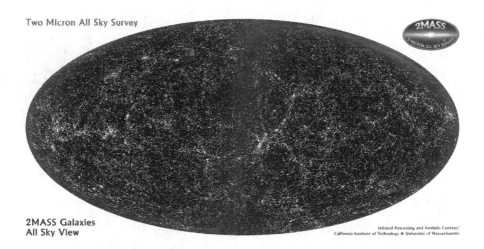

Figure. 1. All sky image. Credits NASA/JPL/ CalTecTwo micron All Sky Survey/ Development Team

Secular cosmologists often use a visual model called the "Raisin Bread" or "Raisin Cake" analogy. In order to show that all galaxies are receding from one another and so no galaxy can claim to be near the center of the universe, this approach considers the change in position of raisins relative to each other in raisin bread during baking. The raisins in the bread move away from each other as the loaf expands. However, consider a real slice of raisin bread in Figure 2.

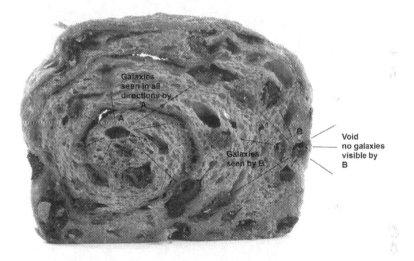

Figure. 2. Slice of raisin bread showing void of raisins at the margin on the right. Image source is FoodPhotoSite. com, (http://www.foodphotosite.com/index.pip : Used by permission).

If one raisin (A) observes as indicated, it sees a relatively uniform distribution of raisins around itself, but a raisin near the edge of the bread (B) sees a large void in the direction of the edge nearest to itself. That there is no large void in any direction around Earth suggests that Earth is at or close to the center of the universe.

Conclusions

Although the Bible is not a scientific textbook and pertains primarily to the sacrifice of our Lord and Savior Jesus Christ for our sins and for the salvation of our souls, it contains verses that are scientific in nature. Two scientific references are those relating to the ocean currents and atmospheric pressure.

The Big Bang theory contains many flaws, including the lack of a center for the universe and the theory that the universe created itself out of nothing. I conclude that observational data and logical assumptions indicate that the universe does have a center.

If you can believe something created itself out of nothing, why is it so difficult to believe that God created the universe and everything in it? It is easier for me to accept the biblical account that an omnipotent God created the universe by the power of His word than to assume that the universe essentially created itself. In the final analysis, the conclusion is that the Bible depicts creation as outlined in Genesis to be a true and accurate description of the beginning of our universe, our earth, and life as we know it.

"Woe to me if I do not preach the Gospel."
(1 Cor. 9:16 NIV)

"But how can a mortal be righteous before God? He alone stretches out the heavens and treads on the waves of the sea. He is the Maker of the Bear and Orion, the Pleiades and the constellations of the South." (Job 9:2, 8, and 9 NIV)

CHAPTER 2

The Cosmic Microwave Background Radiation (CMB)
A Different Perspective

Introduction

The Big Bang model has been used for some time as the primary secular model for cosmology. However, in the simple biblical model the universe is fully formed and functional at creation, as told in Genesis 1:14–19. Penzias and Wilson's 1964 discovery of cosmic microwave background radiation has been used as a "proof" of the Big Bang model. The theory is that the initial, infinitely hot temperatures of the universe has cooled over time to the current background temperature of 2.735° Kelvin, but consider an opposite scenario and ask how long it would take for the margin of the universe to *heat* to a temperature of 2.735° Kelvin. We present an opposite but simple model of cosmic background radiation that shows a young universe.

The Perspective

In the Big Bang model, since the universe began as an infinitely hot and infinitesimally small singularity, the background temperature was achieved theoretically by the expansion of the universe from the initial "bang" and resultant cooling over time to form the universe as we know it today. This secular view of the universe estimates its age at approximately 13.7 billion years, with cooling to the background temperature over this long period of time.

However, the Bible gives a different narrative of the creation of the universe, formed by an omniscient and omnipotent God, who tells us in Genesis 1:14–19 that the sun, the moon, and the stars were created on the fourth day. The possibility of a young universe *must* be considered in light of the biblical narrative. In this chapter I will attempt to show that a young universe is possible by reversing the process of cooling of the universe after the Big Bang to heating of the universe following creation.

Biblical CMB Model

To construct a model for the cosmic background, I employ the current cosmological assumptions that have been made about the structure of the universe and add some assumptions. To begin with, I used the assumptions made by the Friedman-Lemaitre-Robertson-Walker metric that the universe is spatially homogeneous and isotropic. These assumptions are, in essence, a statement of the Cosmological Principle.[1] Therefore, my first assumption is that stars are uniformly distributed throughout the universe.

At this point, let me state that I consider the Cosmological Principle to be an erroneous concept, but for the purposes of this chapter and these calculations, I use the concepts that have been put forth by our secular friends to show, based on their own assumptions and conclusions, that a young universe is also possible, because the biblical model is based on the young universe postulate and subsequent mathematical calculations.

My second assumption is that the sun is representative of an average star in the universe. Certainly there are larger, smaller, hotter, and cooler stars, but the sun is one of the main sequence stars as represented by secular science. Therefore, the radius of our average star is 6.96×10^8 meters, with a surface temperature of approximately 5780° Kelvin. Given the volume of the universe and the estimated number of stars in the universe, the average stellar density is estimated at approximately one star for every cubic billion light years.[2] If a star is placed in the center of this volume, the average star is approximately five hundred light years from the edge of the universe.

My third assumption for the discussion here is that the universe was created with an interstitial temperature of 0° Kelvin, that is, with essentially zero entropy. Moreover, this created star is approximately 4.7305×10^{18} meters from the edge of the universe, and this edge was 0° K and has stayed at 0°. I assume that the current estimate for the size of the universe is a radius of approximately 46.6 billion light years, and the universe is essentially spherical and bounded, one of several secular scenarios.

A primary assumption is that the universe is young, and I make an attempt to show that this is a valid assumption by means of a heat-transfer calculation. This approach was suggested previously by considering heat generation in the early universe,[3] although the article that suggests it appears to be a creation process that indicates a Big Bang. Creation of a mature universe on the fourth day does not exclude the possibility that the interstellar medium was at an initial thermal ground state of 0° Kelvin, at least in the outer portion of the universe, which has progressively heated in the six thousand years since creation.

I use the formula $a_0 + b_0 (\log L) = °$ Kelvin, where L is the radial distance. With r1 the radius of the star, r2 the radius from the center of the model star to the margin of the universe described by the cosmic background radiation temperature, and r3 the radius from the center of the star to the edge of the universe, the model is diagrammed in

Figure 1. Given the radius of the star and the radius to the edge of the universe from this star, the radial distance to the CMB temperature is calculated as 4.6268×10^{18} meters.[4]

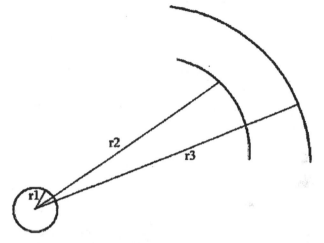

Not to scale

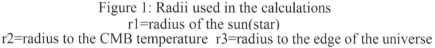

Figure 1: Radii used in the calculations
r1=radius of the sun(star)
r2=radius to the CMB temperature r3=radius to the edge of the universe

Using the standard heat conduction differential equation:

$$\partial^2 u\,(x,\,t)/\partial x^2 = 1\,/\alpha^2\,(\partial u(x,\,t)/\partial t$$

Then splitting the dependent-independent variable, the equation becomes:

$$u(x,\,t) = v(x,\,t) - \varphi\,(x)$$

The next step is to solve this equation for the variable time t, looking for a time that indicates a young universe. The

F. Carlyle Stebner

formulation used and the results obtained, are shown in figure 2.[5] The calculation was done using Maplesoft™.

$$B = \left(2/\left(4.6268 \times 10^{18}\right)\right)\left(-2.735\right) \int_0^{4.6268 \times 10^{18}} \left(\sin\left(\left(\pi\right)/\left(4.6268\right.\right.\right.$$
$$\left.\left.\left.\times 10^{18}\right)\right)\right) \times \left(6.96 \times 10^8\right) dx$$

$\xrightarrow{\text{solve for B}}$ [[B = 9.451666 x 10^{-10}]]

$$2.735 = 2\left(9.451666 \times 10^{-10}\right) \sum_{n=0}^{100000} \left(\cos(n)(\pi)\left(4.6268 \times 10^{18}\right)/\left(6.96\right.\right.$$
$$\left.\times 10^8\right)\right) \times e^{\left(\left(\left(9.633 \times 10^{18}\right)(n)(\pi)/\left(4.6268 \times 10^{18}\right)\right)^2\right)t} - \left(5780\right.$$
$$+ 5780\left(4.6268 \times 10^{18}/6.96 \times 10^8\right)\right)$$

$\xrightarrow{\text{solve for t}}$ [[t = 25.83288368]]

$e^{(25.83288)}/\left(3.1536 \times 10^7\right) = 5251.34593$

Figure 2. Calculations performed indicating a time of 5251 years to increase the border temperature of the universe to the CMB temperature. (3.1536×10^7= number of seconds in one year).

As these calculations indicate, the time required to increase the temperature close to the edge of our spherical universe to the CMB temperature is approximately 5,251years. This result certainly indicates a young universe. However, the calculations are sensitive to initial conditions, as the formula is an exponential power formula.

The parameter α (thermal diffusivity) is calculated from:

α = k (thermal conductivity) / ρ (density)
× c_p (specific heat capacity)

The values for thermal conductivity and specific heat capacity are obtained from Bates,[6] figures 3 and 6. Although other values can be used for these parameters, those chosen for this calculation are 0.800 for thermal conductivity and 49.608 for specific heat capacity. The density is calculated to be 1.674×10^{-21} given an estimated density of one atom of hydrogen per cubic centimeter. These parameters result in a calculated value of 9.633×10^{18} m^2/s.

A similar conclusion was reported in a 1981 paper by Akridge and Barnes,[7] in which the authors used a "Heating Model" to conclude that the maximum age of the Milky Way is approximately 6,800 years. They also indicated that the intergalactic gas does not appear to be very "hot"; however, as we consider the galaxy to be essentially the same age as the universe, these calculations provide a value in the same ballpark as our biblical model predicts. Therefore, a similar conclusion can be drawn, derived by a different method. In addition, the approach presented in this chapter is applicable to the universe as a whole, so this heat-transfer biblical model has a more general application, with similar results.

Conclusions

This chapter has shown an opposite approach to what is known as the Big Bang Theory. This approach is as valid as any Big Bang cooling scenario fostered by the secular cosmology community and is contrary to that presented by the Big Bang model.

The main conclusion that can be drawn from the calculations presented in this chapter is that we are living in a young, created universe. The Bible is correct in saying "the heavens declare the glory of God, and the skies proclaim the work of his hands" (Psalm 19:1 NIV).

"Do not be wise in your own eyes; fear the
Lord and shun evil. (Prov. 3:7 NIV)

"Your word is a lamp to my feet and a light for my path. I have taken an oath and confirmed it, that I will follow your righteous laws." (Psalm 119:105–106 NIV)

"The fear of the Lord is the beginning of knowledge." (Prov. 1:7 NIV)

CHAPTER 3

There Is No Such Thing as "Dark Matter" (or "Dark Energy" either)

Introduction

The Teaching Company's lecture series by Sean Carroll (senior research associate at the California Institute of Technology) uses the phrase "dark energy is especially a mystery" and points out that the study of dark energy may "teach us about fundamental physics."[1] The calculations performed and conclusions reached here regarding this mystery are based on a young universe postulate, so dark matter and dark energy may not be so mysterious after all. Evaluation is also based on an application of fundamental physics concepts and basic calculations, but the main foundation for a simple biblical cosmological model is the Holy Bible, which tells us that an omnipotent God was the prime mover who created the universe, not a universe that created itself out of nothing. Since then, God has governed the universe with His natural laws, which he put in place at creation.

The Fundamental Problem

When Einstein was formulating his General Theory of Relativity, his view was that the universe was static, neither expanding nor contracting. This view led him to introduce the Cosmological Constant (Λ, a fudge factor) into his field equations.[2] When Edwin Hubble discovered that the universe is expanding; Einstein declared that his Cosmological Constant was a mistake.[3]

More recent observations led to an unexpected discovery: that the universe is not only expanding but accelerating.[4] This discovery then led to a rebirth of the Cosmological Constant, as the discovery implies a force that would cause this acceleration—that is, a positive constant. The Cosmological Constant represents the energy necessary to drive this expansion. The simplest possibility for this unknown energy is the energy found in interstellar space, the "vacuum energy" or "dark energy."[5]

Many values have been published for this vacuum energy. In the lecture series on dark energy, Carroll gives the value at 1×10^{-8} ergs/cm^3.[6] Other values include 6.471×10^{-10} ergs/cm^3 and 1.365×10^{-11} ergs/cm^3 (Tipler, 1987 and Question Number 52 ScienceNet Questions and Answers).[7]

However the question concerning what dark matter and dark energy are remains. What in the Bible can shed some light on this question? One of the postulates is a young age for the universe. Matter and energy may be converted according to Einstein's famous $E = mc^2$ equation. Once a conversion has occurred, the energy is not lost but resides in the matter created, or vice versa. The Bible tells us that creation was complete at the end of creation week, when all stars, galaxies, and any remaining gas, dust, and energy, if any, were present. Stellar activity is a primary source of energy in the universe, so the calculations done in this chapter use current energy sources, including stellar activity. Other sources of energy may also be present, but the total mass-energy content created for the universe remains constant.

Finding the information necessary to calculate the total power output of the universe presents some difficulty. Various sources provide differing data, although most give a similar range of information, but not necessarily in the form required for direct analysis. Therefore, reformatting some data is necessary.

Dark Matter

This section begins with a theoretical discussion of "exotic dark matter." Dark matter, as Carmelli noted, is used to explain the observed rotation velocity of galaxies, which is higher than expected[8]—that is, there is a difference between theoretical calculations and the measured rotation velocity of galaxies. Carmelli presented a theoretical treatise called Cosmological General Relativity (CGR). In testing this theory against observational data, the conclusion drawn is that "there is no need for any dark matter to account for the SNe Ia redshift magnitude data. Furthermore, since the predicted transition red shift ... is well within the red shift range of the data, the expansion rate evolution from deceleration to acceleration ... is explained without the need for any dark energy."[9] Therefore, there is theoretically no need for the dark matter or dark energy proposed by secular cosmologists.

In addition to this theoretical conclusion, dark matter, as such, means only that matter is not seen or, more specifically, does not give off any intrinsic detectable radiation that is visible from Earth. However, it is also becoming increasingly evident that there is material in the universe that gives off radiation at wavelengths not detectable by Earth-based telescopes in the infrared and x-ray portion of the electromagnetic spectrum.

Recently, a report from NASA[10] on data from the Chandra X-ray Observatory revealed a halo of hot gas around the Milky Way. This gas cloud appears to extend out to about a 300,000-light-year radius. Other studies reported by NASA have shown that there is hot gas around other galaxies.[11] Thus, so-called dark matter is not dark after all but observable. Therefore, "dark matter" does not appear to be theoretically necessary and is becoming increasingly evident as detectable matter, given the proper equipment to see it.

Dark Energy

In his book[12], Appendix 1: The large-scale structure of the universe does not need 'dark' matter or 'dark' energy; Hartnett stated that these two theoretical constructs are unnecessary. Specifically, Hartnett wrote, "We'll see also, in Appendices 2 and 4, that 'dark' energy is not needed in the theory to make it fit observations. … In the CGR theory, this is the energy of the vacuum, the stuff that space is made of."

Continuing the discussion of cosmology, we find that the concept of dark energy is contained in the Cosmological Constant (Λ), Einstein's "fudge factor." As Carroll stated, "The terms 'cosmological constant' and 'vacuum energy' are essentially interchangeable."[13] In addition, remember also that: "Cosmological observations imply, $|\rho_\Lambda^{(obs)}| \leq (10^{-12}\text{GeV})^4 \sim 10^{-8}\text{erg/cm}^3$."[14]

Since one major source of energy in the universe is stellar, the bolometric luminosity of Sol, as an average stellar energy output of the stars in the universe, is used for analysis. Hot gases in galaxies and between clusters and super clusters also provide energy, as do quasars. Galactic stellar activity is included in the stars category.[15] The galactic gas energy output is summarized in Table 1.

Galaxy Type	Energy Output Erg/sec	References
Spiral	8.827×10^{75}	Savage, 1987[16] Pogge, 2006[17]
Elliptical	6.226×10^{77}	Darling[18] Barstow,200S[19]
Irregular	1.286×10^{75}	Pogge,2006[20] Korista[21]
Average Number of Galaxies	$1.1S \times 10^{11}$	Mackie, 1999[22] Murray, 1999[23]
Average Power Density	2.109×10^{77}	

Table 1: Intragalactic Gas Energy Output

Table 2 shows the contribution of each energy source and the calculation of the total power output. The average energy output is calculated using the values from the data available, and the calculation of the energy from hot gas is done by simplifying on the geometric basis. Spiral galaxies are viewed as a flat cylinder, elliptical and irregular galaxies are viewed as spheres, and intra-galactic cluster gas is viewed as a thin, flat cylinder or sheet. I understand that intergalactic gas is found in sheets, ribbons, and rivers, with irregular shapes and distributions. Other sources of energy that are present in the universe, such as the lengthening of the wavelength of light, do not add sufficient energy to affect these calculations.

Source	Energy Output Ergs/sec	References
Stars	3.846×10^{56}	Chaisson, 2005[24] ESA, 2004[25]
Galactic Gas	2.109×10^{77}	Table I
Intracluster Gas	1.369×10^{69}	New World Encyclopedia, 2009[26]
Super Cluster Gas	7.862×10^{73}	Keel, 2009[27] Economic Expert, 2011[28] Paerels, 2010[29]
Quasars	2×10^{52}	Wikipedia, 2011[30]
Average Output	4.220×10^{76}	
Volume of Universe	3×10^{86} cm^3	Wikipedia, 2011[31]
Average Power Density per sec Output	1.406×10^{-10} Ergs/cm^3/s	

Table 2: Energy Sources in the Universe.

As Table 2 shows, the calculation of the average power density is close to the estimated vacuum energy density. The power output is based on a number of assumptions, such as the geometric simplifications used and the number of galaxies that contain hot gas; moreover, I suspect somewhat incomplete data at this stage of exploration of the universe. These numbers, as well as the measured energy density, may change with future discoveries. However, as an initial approximation, the numbers are reasonably close to the vacuum energy density.

Quantum Theory Considerations

If Quantum Theory is used, the energy density of the vacuum should be infinite, but this energy density is not what is measured. Calculating the vacuum energy using Plank scale units results in an energy density value of 2×10^{110} ergs/cm^3, but observations give a cosmological constant of approximately 2×10^{-10} ergs/cm^3, as reported by Carroll,[32] or 1×10^{-8}, also reported by Carroll. It seems logical to conclude that the energy contributed by the quantum fluctuations of the vacuum is not a factor or that the application of Quantum Theory to the universe needs to be fine-tuned.

Young Universe Considerations

In order to evaluate a biblical creation model, Table 3 shows different measurements for the universe for reference:

	Created Universe	Current Universe	Larger Universe
Volume	7.571×10^{59} m^3	3.60×10^{80} m^3	7.83×10^{88} m^3
Radius	5.684×10^{19} m	4.41×10^{26} m	2.65×10^{29} m

Table 3: Comparison of three radii and volumes referred to in the text.

Comparing the calculations for the energy output of the universe to the value given for dark energy reveals a striking similarity. Granted, there are different values published for this dark energy—most likely the vacuum energy density (or Λ). Carroll is correct in stating that "vacuum energy does not change as the universe expands."[33] In this simple biblical cosmological model, I postulate that the relatively constant vacuum energy is most likely because the energy in the universe is constantly being replaced, maintained by the continuous energy output by stars and hot gas.

Since the calculated average power density is essentially the same as the vacuum energy density, a simple calculation shows that only a short time is required to attain this energy level. Dividing the average power output by the volume of observed universe gives an average power density of 1.406×10^{-10} ergs/cm^3 for each second of power output. This calculated power density is smaller than the measured value (the baseline value in this biblical model—as given by Carroll—of 1×10^{-8} erg/cm^3) and significantly less than the results of the quantum theory calculations. Taking into account the accommodation coefficient, calculated to be 0.35, [34] the average power density is 4.921×10^{-11} ergs/cm^3.[35] The energy density given by Carroll would then take approximately 203 seconds to attain, given these calculations.

A spin-off calculation using this approach is also revealing. The radiation energy density in equilibrium "considering that the universe is filled with black body radiation at a temperature of 2.7° K" is reported to be "0.25 MeV/m^3."

[36] This calculation results in an energy density of 4.005×10^{-19} ergs/cm^3.

Using the value of stellar power output only (Table 2) for a period of 9,900 years gives a calculated energy density of 4.005×10^{-19} ergs/cm^3, a value identical to that reported by Nave[36]. This value confirms again a young universe, as opposed to the secular estimate of 13.7 billion years.

Dark energy has been a controversial issue in cosmology for some time. Vacuum energy density is considered a likely candidate for this "dark energy". I concur with this evaluation, so I postulate that the power output of the universe as a whole is supplying this energy. The measurement of the energy density may be the measure of this power output over the time for which these measurements were obtained. I also postulate that, as the vacuum density increases, the pressure from this increase causes the universe to expand, which produces a decrease in the energy density that is then resupplied by the continued power output of the universe itself.

However, another implication to this approach is the size of the universe. As we have seen, the theoretical energy density of the universe is more than that measured. We assume the value of 1×10^{-8} ergs/cm^3 provided by Carroll to be an upper limit.

Take the number of seconds in a year (3.1536×10^7 seconds) and multiply this number by the baseline young age of the universe (6,000 years) for a total time of 1.892×10^{11} seconds. Then multiply this time by the average power output of the universe, and divide the product by the volume of the universe in cubic centimeters, giving a result of 26.25 ergs/cm^3. This value is larger than the measured energy density in the observable universe but much less than the value obtained by quantum theory calculations. Dividing the calculated power density by the measured power density given by Carroll results in a ratio of 2.625×10^9 to1, indicating the possibility that the size of the universe is 2.625×10^9 times larger than that which has been estimated. Multiplying this figure by the current estimated volume of the universe gives a value of 7.833×10^{95} cm^3.

Consequently, the volume of the universe may be as large as 7.833×10^{95} cm^3, although the exact size of the universe is unknown. Guth suggests that "the size of the universe was about equal to the speed of light times its age or perhaps even larger. ... [W]e find that the entire universe is expected to be at least 10^{23} times larger than the observed universe."[37] Thus, the calculation presented here of the size of the universe as relates to the simple biblical cosmological model is well within the size Guth suggested.

Using the energy density with the total average power output of 4.22×10^{76} ergs/sec for six thousand years, gives a total power output of 1.331×10^{84} ergs and a calculated energy density of 4.44×10^{-3} ergs/cm³. Based on a larger universe, this value would result in an energy density of 1.88×10^{-12} ergs/cm³, which is close to the value given in Cheng of 1.365×10^{-11} ergs/cm³ [38]. Thus, a number of calculations based on the measured energy density and a larger universe than is visible are consistent with a young universe.

Gravity and Pressure Considerations

For the gravity evaluations, consider two scenarios and which, if any, correlate with measured values: 1) A straight Newtonian gravity calculation and 2) for those who love relativity, a relativistic calculation. Both use two variations of mass/energy content of the universe. If the postulate is that there is no such entity as dark energy, then the total mass content of the universe can be used, but the total mass/ energy estimate in the observable universe will also be used for two subsequent calculations in order to evaluate and compare this approach. However, an estimate for the total mass/energy of the larger universe is not available in the secular literature. In addition, if the total mass/energy of the universe is used as a basis for calculations, any additional gravitation that relativistic cosmologists say is generated by the pressure of the interstitial energy content of the universe itself is already included in the total mass/ energy number. Either a total mass/energy value is used or not. If an additional factor for the pressure generated by the interstitial energy density is used, then the gravitational potential of the universe is going to be larger than the values given for the total mass/energy present.

Instead of looking at the expansion of the universe as being due to an unknown "dark energy," we should reconsider and revise this secular theory. The postulate of our biblical model is that the energy for expansion is the positive pressure, secondary to the energy density that is present in the universe as a whole. This energy density produces an internal pressure on the margin of the universe, causing expansion or, more specifically, a pressure gradient between the "inside" of the universe and the "outside," which we assume produces no opposing pressure—that is, the external pressure is zero.

However, in the context of the universe as a whole, is the relativistic formula the correct one to use? For those who study Einstein's theories, I think the answer would be a resounding *yes*, but I suggest that a relativistic formula is not applicable to the universe neither as a whole nor to the edge of the universe, on which our current discussion focuses.

The Einstein equation can be written as:

$$R_{\mu\nu} - 1/2Rg_{\mu\nu} + \Lambda g_{\mu\nu} = (8\pi G/c^4)\, T_{\mu\nu}\,^{39}$$

Einstein himself introduced a fudge factor (Λ) to make his equation do what he wanted it to do. (The addition of a fudge factor should make all physicists happy, since even Einstein used one in his formula.) However, after the formula was evaluated further, the universe described was determined to be unstable.[40] Therefore, on the face of it, the formula Einstein proposed was flawed since it did not accurately describe the universe as a whole since, "The cosmological constant term was originally introduced by Einstein to allow for a stable universe (i.e., one that is not expanding or contracting). The effort was unsuccessful for two reasons: the static universe described by this theory was unstable, and observations of distant galaxies by Hubble a decade later confirmed that our universe is, in fact, not static but expanding. So Λ was abandoned, with Einstein calling it the 'biggest blunder [he] ever made.' For many years the cosmological constant was almost universally considered to be zero."[41]

The question, then, concerns what the cosmological constant was supposed to do. What was its function that Einstein felt it necessary to add a fudge factor? The thought at the time was that the universe was constant in size. So, "From his General Theory of Relativity, Einstein constructed a cosmological explanation of the universe, based on a four – dimensional space-time metric. He saw that with this model the universe would tend to collapse under gravitation, so he added a constant (represented by the Greek symbol lambda (Λ)) to his field equations, to maintain a static universe."[42]

Therefore, Einstein was essentially wrong in his formulation of a geometric explanation for gravity for the universe as a whole. It is evident that extending his theory to the universe is an overextension in the same way that overextension of the Copernican Principle to the universe as a whole rather than limiting use of the principle to the solar system is erroneous. In the same way the Cosmological Principle is applied erroneously because the universe is not uniform but heterogeneous in the evident distribution of galaxies and stars. Secular cosmologists use these principles in trying to eliminate God from cosmology. However, these cosmologists forget that God defined and put in place the very predictable natural laws that are present in the universe today.

Does the use of a fudge factor mean that Einstein's equations are irrelevant? Absolutely not, but the validity of the theory is observable in local phenomena, and is not necessarily applicable to the universe as a whole. For example, the effect that Einstein's equations define in their application are seen in calculations of the perihelion of Mercury, the visual bending of light around the sun, and the large accumulation of galaxies that result in gravitational lensing, which is secondary to the large but still local gravitational phenomenon.

Then why do I say that general relativity is a local phenomenon? Einstein's equation has always been described as a geometric explanation of gravity. The main evidence of the theory's correctness is in local observations, such as that you and I stick to the surface of the earth.

What about the universe as a whole? The most recent evaluation related to the geometry of the universe is that it is flat, that is, that the geometry is Euclidean. This idea is easily visualized with the famous balloon model that secular science often uses to illustrate the expanding universe, with galaxies stuck to the surface of the balloon.

However, galaxies are not on the surface of the balloon but inside, in the universe itself. The surface of the balloon may be spherical, but the inside can still be Euclidean, with parallel lines always parallel from point to point throughout the interior of the balloon. There are local distortions of the space inside the balloon that are due to local gravitational effects, but the overall internal volume is linear.

With the biblical creation model I propose a spherical universe, where the surface of the universe is curved, but any small section of the surface is, for all practical purposes, flat. And, the interior is flat, that is Euclidean.

Another view of the surface of the universe is that of a soccer ball. With this model, each panel of the surface is essentially flat. I refer to "a new study of astronomical data, only recently available, hints at a possible answer [to the question of the shape of the universe]. The universe is finite and bears a rough semblance to a soccer ball or, more accurately, a dodecahedron, a 12-sided volume bounded by pentagons." According to freelance mathematician Jeffrey Weeks, "'What makes it exciting now is it's not a matter of idle speculation.'" [43] I like this shape for a cosmological model also, since secular cosmologists accept that the universe is flat. With this cosmological model, the surface portions of the universe are relatively flat; at least the pentagon sections that overall form a spherical shape.

An article on WMAP data also states that "the contents [WMAP measurements] point to a 'flat' Euclidean geometry, with the ratio of the energy density in curvature to the critical density being $0.0179 < \Omega_k < 0.0081$ (95% CL). The WMAP measurements also support a cosmic inflation paradigm in several ways, including the flatness measurements."[44] Einstein's geometry is a curved geometry, essentially pseudo-Riemannian. However, as I have shown, the current data support the conclusion that the universe is Euclidian in nature.

In order to evaluate gravitational potential and pressure further, nonrelativistic particles should be considered in a relativistic expansion of space itself. However, nonrelativistic particles are still nonrelativistic.

In answer to the question concerning why pressure is a source of gravity, theoretical physicist Lubos Motl, in part, stated that, "for low velocities, the dominant complement of the equation [Einstein's field equations] is the $\mu\nu = 00$ (time – time) component, and it effectively reduces to $\Delta\varphi_{grav} = 4\,\pi\,G\rho$, the Poisson equation for Newton's gravity, which implies all the inverse square distance law, and so on." Mathematical physicist Lawrence B. Crowell provided another answer, saying in part, "The contribution of pressure to the curvature occurs if the motion of the molecules is relativistic."[45] The biblical model, then, must take into account the thermodynamic considerations near $0°$ Kelvin. At temperatures nearing zero, nearly all molecular motion ceases, and $\Delta S = 0$ for any adiabatic process, where S is the entropy. In such circumstances, pure substances can (ideally) form perfect crystals as $T \rightarrow 0°$ K. I postulate that this is what is happening at the external surface of the universe, where a thin layer of ice crystals has formed. This concept has already been proposed by creationist author Russell Humphreys.[46]

Taking these concepts as postulates, I submit that the velocity of particles that impart a pressure, as in a gas, is not relative at temperatures near absolute $0°$ Kelvin.[47] Space may be expanding relativistically, and our secular colleagues admit the fabric of space can expand faster than the speed of light—super relativistically if you prefer. Matter cannot have a velocity faster than that of light, but the fabric of space is a different matter. In any event, molecules near the edge of the universe are not considered to be relativistic particles (because of the temperature in this location), so they do not contribute to the gravitational potential at the edge of the universe.

Relativity Considerations

Consider the following analysis of Einstein's general relativity equation as it applies to the Big Bang Theory. If mass-energy distorts space-time and if the pressure of relativistic particles related to the Big Bang also contributes to gravity, then when a singularity of infinitely small size and infinite mass starts to expand, the relativistic particles would contribute more gravitation than the mass and the energy equivalent of the mass do. Therefore, one would think that the pressure of relativistic particles, which also contribute to gravity, would contribute more gravity such that the rapid expansion of the universe (the Big Bang) would never occur. This is another nail in the Big Bang coffin and more support for a created universe.

If the concept of special relativity is correct, then all energy has a mass equivalent, so, according to Einstein, *any* energy present in the universe would contribute to a gravitational potential[48] and, consequently, would not be repulsive. Cosmologist Sean Carroll supports this interpretation of general relativity as well in stating that, "in general relativity … all energy couples to gravity …."[49]

Therefore, either Einstein's Theory of Relativity is wrong or the notion that "dark energy" causes the expansion of the universe is wrong. To paraphrase an old proverb, "You can't have your relativity and eat it too."

To look at a repulsive force another way, if secular cosmologists are willing to accept the idea of a repulsive "exotic dark energy" that opposes general relativity, then the concept of expansion of space itself that does not produce a gravitational potential as being due to the will of God should not be difficult to accept in the biblical model of cosmology.

Gravity Plots

Next, I use two methods of calculating gravity and plot the results with the pressure exerted on the margin of the universe from the interstitial energy density present. Also needed is a determination of the pressure (in Pascals) that the energy density exerts on the interior surface of the universe. Switching to the International System of Units of measure, that is, meters, seconds and kilograms, will be helpful.

At this point you may well ask how one knows that the radius of the created universe is 5.684×10^{19} m. One of the main postulates in the model of biblical cosmology is that the universe was created at a finite size by an omnipotent God six thousand years ago (as a baseline for the biblical model). One of the Hubble space telescope's more recent detections is a distant galaxy with a tentative redshift of between 10.3 and 11.9.[50] Since this source of light was detected recently, the time postulate in the biblical model, is that the light from this galaxy started traveling a little more than six thousand years ago. The radius for 6013 light years is 5.684×10^{19} meters, which suggests a minimum radius at the time of creation. As time goes by and more distant galaxies are detected, the evidence for the minimum radius at creation expands with the new information, rather than being limited by it. In my opinion, this postulate eliminates the need for black or white holes to determine the origin of the universe from a biblical standpoint, and the creation of a mature universe by an omnipotent God becomes a straightforward process.

A second question you may ask concerns how to justify using only Newtonian gravity, which is the law of universal gravitation, to calculate the gravitational force of the universe at its edge. Mathematically:

$$F = G \, (m_1 m_2 / r^2),$$

where G equals Newton's gravitational constant, m1 and m2 are two gravitationally attracted masses, and r is the distance between them. I refer you to an article by Korean astronomers Hwang and Noh, which states, "As we prove that the Newtonian hydrodynamic equations are valid in all cosmological scales to second order, and that the third-order correction terms are small, our result has the important practical implication that one can now use the large-scale Newtonian numerical simulation more reliably as the simulation scale approaches and even goes beyond the horizon."[51] With the previous discussion of the lack of relativistic particles at low temperature, I believe that the calculations presented in this chapter are valid in the 1 m³ of space to which they are applied at the edge of the universe. To simplify the calculations I also postulate that the mass of ice crystals in 1 m² at the margin of the universe is 1 kg.

However, in order not to disappoint our relativistic friends, I also provide a calculation based on general relativity and include the pressure that the energy density produces in this one cubic meter of space using the formula:

$$g = (4\pi/3)\ G\ (\rho + 3P/c^2)\ r,$$

where g is the gravitational attraction on the edge of the universe, G is Newton's gravitational constant, ρ is the matter/energy density, P is the pressure from the energy density[52], c is the speed of light, and r is the radius of the universe.[53] For the biblical creation model calculations, I use the baseline (created) radius for a universe of six thousand light years, or 5.6724×10^{16} km.

Also postulated in the biblical model is that the mass and/ or energy gravitational potential is focused at the center of the universe. This postulate derives from the Shell Theorem, which Isaac Newton proved. This theorem states that "a spherical asymmetric body affects external objects gravitationally as though all of its mass is concentrated at a point in its center."[54]

				Total M+E	M+Dk M	Total M+E	M+Dk M
Interstitial Energy		Pressure		Newtonian		Relativistic	
Density/m³						~	
	t (yrs.)	Joules	Pascals	g (Newtons)	g	g	g
Creation	0	10^{-9}	10^{-9}	6.276×10^{1}	6.214×10^{2}	6.324×10^{4}	6.261×10^{2}
Now	6000	10^{-9}	10^{-9}	1.038×10^{-6}	1.028×10^{-11}	5.156×10^{-9}	4.127×10^{-9}

Table 4: Calculated gravity values in the universe from estimated Total Mass + Energy and Matter + Dark Matter only.

Now, having calculated the parameters for gravity, what about the pressure that drives the expansion of the universe and contributes to its acceleration? Pressure is defined as energy per unit volume[55]:

$$P = E/V$$

Since the energy in one cubic meter of space adjacent to the edge of the universe has already been defined, there are1 × 10^{-9} Joules per cubic meter, which results in a pressure of 1 × 10^{-9} Pascals per square meter against the layer of ice crystals (the waters above)[56] that form the exterior of the margin of the universe. The pressure, which is exerted laterally and proximally, is balanced by the pressure from the adjacent space. The biblical model also assumes that the pressure exterior to this layer of ice crystals is essentially zero. Given these parameters, the gravity and pressure at creation and at six thousand years after creation can now be calculated (Table 4). Note also that the exact energy density of interstitial space at the time of creation is not known. However, to simplify the calculations that follow, the biblical model postulates that the energy density is essentially the same as it is now. Extending into the future, the central postulate of our current discussion is that the energy density is maintained by the energy output of the universe itself, and the energy density is stabilized by the resulting expansion of the universe.

In the discussion of marginal heating of the universe (chapter 2), the assumption was an initial interstitial temperature of 0° Kelvin, at least at the outer margin of the universe. But remember that the previous discussion relates to the temperature change at the margin of the universe from a heat transfer process. In this chapter the focus is on the interstitial energy density of the fabric of space itself. Note also, as shown previously, that only a short time would be necessary to provide the interstitial energy needed to attain a relatively stable energy density.

You can see from the data given above that the gravity parameter at year six thousand still exceeds the pressure parameter but by only a small amount. A graph can now be constructed given the two points—one at creation and one at six thousand years after creation (or AD 2000)—as a linear plot. As the universe enlarges, the gravitational potential of the universe decreases, and assuming the energy density of the universe remains constant, the energy density plot remains essentially flat (constant), which also simplifies the biblical model. Figure 1 shows the year at which the gravity lines cross the energy line, which I interpret as the point at which the universe stops slowing down and begins to expand again as the interstitial energy (and hence pressure) exceeds the gravitational potential. The graph shows two of the calculated gravity values, and then the lines are extrapolated down to the energy line, as shown.

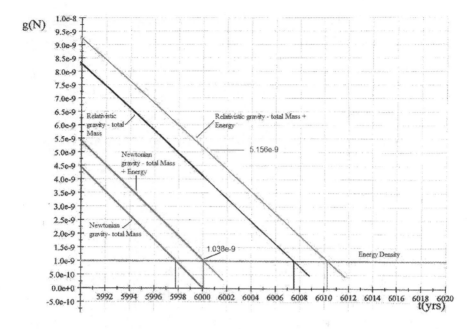

Figure 1: Detailed graph produced using Scientific WP of the gravity curves as they converge and cross the vacuum energy density curve (equated to Pascals). Total mass includes visible mass plus dark matter estimates; + energy indicates the inclusion of the mass equivalent of the energy in the universe, including estimates of dark energy.

Now we correlate these calculations and curves to experimental data. The initial study that demonstrated evidence of an accelerating universe was reported in1998.[57] This discovery correlates most closely with the Newtonian gravity line in Figure 1, indicating that acceleration of the universe may have started toward the end of 1997. Also note that this line includes the calculation of gravity using Newton's universal gravitation formula and only the mass equivalent of visible mass plus dark matter. As discussed, dark matter is probably related to hot gas that emits wavelengths in the infrared region that are not well seen from Earth but are visible from observational satellites. In this regard, secular estimates of so-called dark matter can logically be included in the calculations and plotted graphs.

Conclusions

An omnipotent God created the universe, created at a finite size, smaller at creation than estimated now, as a mature universe, with stars and galaxies formed at the time of creation. However, the current size of the universe may be as much as a billion times larger than currently estimated.

This chapter demonstrates the postulate proposed at the beginning of the chapter, that a negative dark energy does not exist. The expansion of the universe is driven by pressure from the vacuum energy density of the universe, which will not decrease, as it is maintained by the total energy output of the universe as a whole. Although the exact amount of interstitial energy present at the beginning of creation is unknown, for simplification of these graphs, the energy level is assumed to be similar to that seen now. The conclusion is that only a relatively short time was necessary to achieve these levels, which again indicates a young universe.

Newtonian gravitational calculations are adequate for the purpose of evaluating the gravitational potential in a one-cubic-meter-section of the universe that lies next to the outer margin, and the pressure differential between the inside and outside of the universe is equivalent to the vacuum energy density. All the linear plots shown demonstrate that, after approximately AD 2010, internal pressure exceeds the gravitational potential. The conclusion must be that the universe will continue to expand and at an accelerating rate. This conclusion has been demonstrated by calculating Newtonian gravity as well as relativistic gravity.

The biblical cosmological model also accepts the current secular evaluation of an essentially Euclidean geometry within the universe itself. Although the margin may be spherical, the "soccer ball" concept of the universe in which the panels that make up the edge of the universe are essentially flat, is both acceptable and unique.

Although Einstein's geometry describes the curvature of space and time, this distortion must be considered a local phenomenon, especially if the overall geometry inside the universe is Euclidean. Einstein certainly was a genius in developing the Theory of Relativity. The distortion of time and space in relationship to gravitational bodies has also been demonstrated experimentally.

Similarly, the Copernican principle and the cosmological principle should not be applied to the universe as a whole. Copernicus described the solar system, but the WMAP images clearly show a heterogeneous galaxy distribution, even though secular scientists put a homogeneous spin on the WMAP data.

"For the message of the cross is foolishness to those who are perishing, but to us who are being saved it is the power of God." (1 Cor. 1:18 NIV)

"This is what God the Lord says, He who created the heavens and stretched them out, who spread out the earth and all that comes out of it, who gives breath to its people and life to those who walk on it: 'I, the Lord, have called you in righteousness ....'" (Isaiah 42:5–6 NIV)

CHAPTER 4

The Hubble Parameter

All calculations, curve fitting, and plots in this chapter are performed using Scientific WP.

Introduction

No book that discusses cosmology would be complete without some discussion of the Hubble parameter and the history behind it. The Hubble parameter is also called the Hubble constant, but since the Hubble is dependent on time, it should not be called a constant. A logical beginning point is with Hubble's discovery, which was based on measured redshifts of an astronomical light source, and Hubble's formulation of what is known as Hubble's Law.

The parameters found in Hubble's Law—recession velocity as it relates to the distance to the light source in the universe—are not measured directly. What Hubble found was a proportionality with the redshift measurements (some of which were measured by Vesto Slipher in 1917) and an assumed distance to the light source (e.g., a distant galaxy).

Hubble plotted a linear correlation between redshift on the Y-axis and distance in mega parsecs on the X-axis and obtained from this relationship a value of 500 km/s/Mpc for the Hubble constant. This value was controversial for some time, especially between astronomers Gerard de Vaucouleurs, who said the value of the Hubble parameter should be about 100, and Allan Sandage, who favored a value of about 50.[1]

The early measurements of Hubble's parameter were large compared to the measurements obtained today. Early values ranged from 600, measured by Lemaître in 1927, to 530 and 526, measured by Hubble in 1929 and 1936, respectively.[2] Currently the values range from approximately 65 to about 75 km/s/Mpc,[3] giving an average of approximately 70 km/s/Mpc, although others suggest the possibility of 42 km/s/Mpc.[4]

Calculating the Hubble Curve

There are multiple measurements for the Hubble parameter, but it may be possible to obtain a formula for calculating it beginning with a Hubble parameter of zero at creation and performing a curve fit to a representative sample of the Hubble values obtained recently. I obtained a representative sample of the Hubble values, obtained by various observers, from two graphs published by J. Huchra[5, 6] and tried multiple curve fitting routines using the selected sample (see Table

1). The best result came from using a cubic polynomial curve fit. Using sample data, including early values such as those from Hubble and Lemaître, I obtained a prominent early inflection point, after which the Hubble parameter plot became negative.

Since we are using a cubic equation, you may well ask how one determines a workable formula when the general form of a cubic equation is

$$Y = Ax^3 + Bx^2 + Cx + D$$

and, therefore, there is an infinite number of solutions. The answer is the formula that most closely fits the data that has been measured and produced by the curve-fitting routine. If a calculated formula corresponds relatively well to the measured data points that are used, then one can assume that the formula is a good approximation of the desired goal.

Although the initial formula correlated relatively well to the database used, including the early measured values of H, the plotted curve did not appear to be satisfactory for the simple biblical model since the maximum was large and the curve became negative, so I limited the database to Hubble values measured from 1960 and later. This approach allowed me to use numbers that are considered more accurate than earlier numbers, as the values measured initially are considered by astronomers to be too high. These higher measurements were due to Hubble's misidentifying distant galaxies that were actually star clusters; Hubble had not been observing "standard candles," that is, objects whose absolute luminosity does not vary with the distance from Earth.[7]

The database is shown in Table 1, the plot of the modified curve is shown in Figure 1, and coned-down views are shown in Figures 2 and 3. Figure 4 shows the plot of the first derivative of the Hubble curve, which calculates the maximum and minimum points of the curve.

t	H	t	H	t	H	t	H
0	0	5976	90	5985.5	120	6001	72
5960	150	5976.2	77	5985.6	68	6002	80
5963.5	100	5977	84	5986.5	72	6006	77
5964	125	5978	75	5987	72.5	6007	71
5968	100	5979	100	5987.5	55	6009	74
5969	110	5979.1	57	5988.5	85	6010	71
5970	90	5980	80	5989	70	6010.5	72.6
5971	50	5980.5	96	5990	72	6011	74
5972	55	5981	55	5990.5	80		
5972.5	95	5982	72	5991	45		
5972.6	41	5983	82	5995	72.6		
5973	40	5984	92	5997	70		
5974	58	5984.5	85	5999	67		
5975	50.5	5985	90	6000	72.5		

Table 1: Data used for Hubble curve fit. Note that 5960 is 1960.

The raw curve fit is:

$$H = 4.0163 \times 10^{-8}\, t^3 - 5.7742 \times 10^{-4}$$
$$t^2 + 2.0303\, t + 6.232 \times 10^{-3}$$

However, if the parameters are modified so the fitted curve matches the data points more closely, a relatively simple polynomial result is:

$$H = 3.288 \times 10^{-8}\, t^3 - 3.96 \times 10^{-4}\, t^2 + 1.2\, t + 30$$

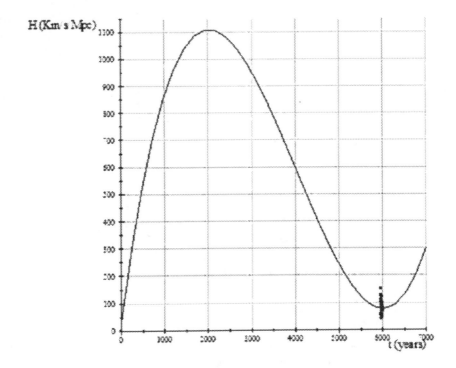

Figure 1: Plot of the modified Hubble curve

As an additional demonstration of the fit of the more recent data points, Figure 2 shows a coned-down view, with the minimum of the curve close to six thousand years after creation (year 2000). This view also demonstrates that the curve is relatively flat from 1950 to 2025.

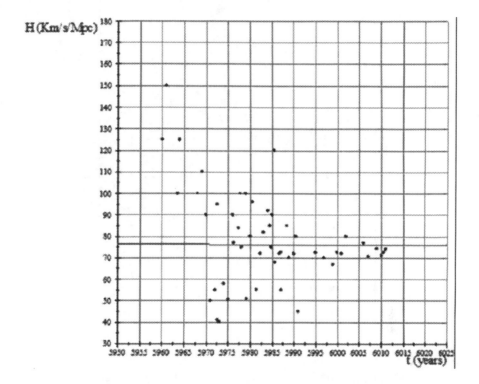

Figure 2: Coned-down view of the larger plot to show the relationship to the selected data points at the minimum.

An additional coned-down view (Figure 3) plotted for the time of creation shows that, according to the calculated Hubble curve, the universe had an initial Hubble value of

30. The next section contains more discussion of the early expansion of the universe.

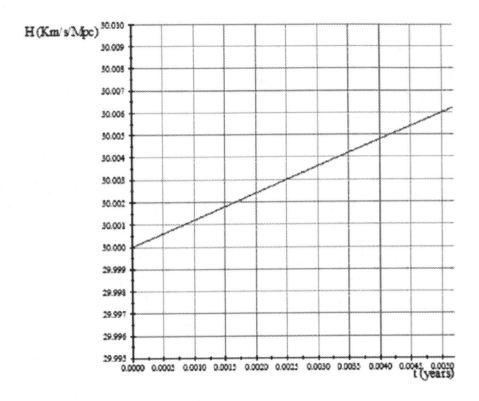

Figure 3: Coned-down view of the time of creation, which demonstrates that the created universe had an initial H value of 30.

The first derivative of this formula is:

$$H' = 9.864 \times 10^{-8} t^2 - 7.92 \times 10^{-4} t + 1.2$$

and the roots are 6008.5 and 2024.7.

Figure 4 is the first derivative of the Hubble curve, which demonstrates the time at which the maximum and minimum occurs. Note that the minimum of the modified curve is calculated to be the year 2008.5.

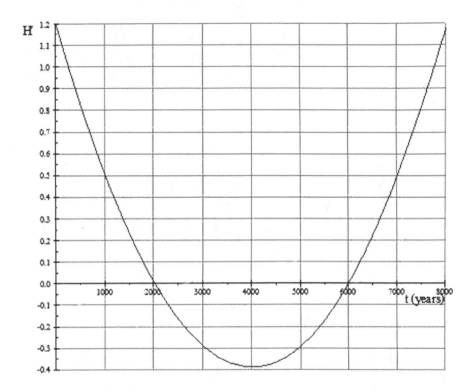

Figure 4: Plot of the first derivative of the Hubble curve, showing the time value at the maximum and minimum inflexion points.

Using the Hubble curve formula to perform several calculations demonstrates how the formula can be used to evaluate other parameters of interest. By inserting the roots of the first derivative into the formula for the time parameter (t), the Hubble value can be calculated at the minimum and maximum of the Hubble curve:

$$H = \frac{3.288 \times 10^{-8} (6008.5)^3 - 3.96 \times 10^{-4}}{(6008.5)^2 + 1.2(6008.5) + 30.}$$

The solution is 76.086 for the Hubble value at the minimum (the year 2008.5). Similarly, the time can be inserted for the maximum of the plotted curve:

$$H = \frac{3.288 \times 10^{-8} (2024.7)^3 - 3.96 \times 10^{-4}}{(2024.7)^2 + 1.2(2024.7) + 30.}$$

The solution is 1109.2, which is the Hubble value at the maximum (the year 1975.3 BC).

The radius of the universe at creation in this simple biblical model is 5.6724×10^{19} m, or 5.6724×10^{16} km. Therefore, $(5.6724 \times 10^{16}) \div (3.09 \times 10^{19}) = 1.835\ 7 \times 10^{-3}$ Mpc., the radius of creation in mega parsecs. At creation, H is 30 km/s/Mpc from the Hubble curve. Calculating velocity at this time, 30 km/s/Mpc $\times$ (1.8357×10^{-3}) Mpc gives a value of 0.0550 71 km/sec.

Calculating the number of seconds in 0.005 years (31,104,000 sec/yr. $\times$ 0.005 yrs.) gives $1.555\ 2 \times 10^5$ seconds, and 1 Mpc $= 3.09 \times 10^{19}$ km. In the first 1.5552×10^5 seconds, the acceleration is 0.055071 km/sec $\div 1.5552 \times 10^5$ sec = 3.5411

$\times$ 10^{-7} km/s/s. This calculation indicates that the initial acceleration of the universe (if present) was low.

Discussion

The goal of the curve-fitting process presented in this chapter is to show that a mathematical formula can be obtained from a database obtained from recent measurements of the Hubble parameter. This formula can then be used to plot a curve, which can then be extrapolated into the past to calculate a Hubble parameter at any time since creation. The database includes values measured up to the year 2011 in order to be at least somewhat inclusive and allows extrapolation into the future as well. Older measurements of the Hubble parameter are excluded, as they appear to be inaccurate.

The first notable aspect of the Hubble curve is that the initial Hubble value is 30 km/s/Mpc. The initial section of the curve, up to the year 2024.7 after the year of creation (Anno Mundi, or AM), indicates that God determined that the universe needed to expand, as I show later. We see a peak at the year AM 2024.7 and a minimum at AD 2008.5.

Also noted from the curve is that, during our current era, the Hubble values are going through a relatively flat portion of this curve. This minimum portion of the curve suggests that during these years, a "quiescent era," there is relatively little change in the measurement of the Hubble parameter. However, the curve predicts that the Hubble parameter will increase in value as the universe expands and will climb rapidly in the future. Therefore, a prediction from the Hubble curve corresponds with the current secular determination of an expanding universe. Of course, it remains to be seen whether this prediction is valid.

The descending portion of the curve does not represent a contraction of the universe but a slowing of expansion and shows a minimum of expansion during the current era. Referring to the earlier discussion of dark matter and dark energy, the minimum calculated point on the curve follows the point at which the relativistic gravity curve calculated from the total mass of the universe (visible and invisible matter) crosses the pressure line from the interstitial energy content of the universe. This comparison suggests two conclusions: The first is that the relativistic gravity line, which does not include "dark energy" but does include the gravity generated by pressure of the energy density in the marginal cubic meter of space, indicates that "dark energy" is the pressure of the interstitial space. The second conclusion is that, as the pressure and gravity equalize, the Hubble parameter stabilizes. As the marginal pressure exceeds the gravitational potential, the universe will begin to expand. I believe this conclusion to be well demonstrated and to be compatible with a young universe model.

For Biblical Scholars

For those who are biblical scholars, I have an additional speculation for your contemplation. The Hubble curve is reproduced with two notations (Figure 5).

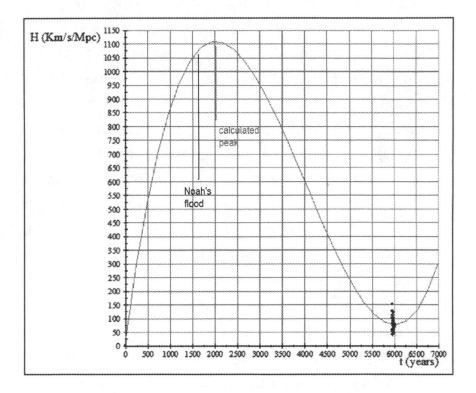

Figure 5: Hubble Curve with notations.

Biblical scholars have suggested that the date of Noah's flood is AM 1656, which is prior to the peak of our Hubble curve. If God decided to judge the world and bring on the worldwide flood at this point, He may also have withdrawn His benevolent expanding of the universe by His mighty power and design. Therefore, the universe continued to expand but less and less rapidly as time progressed. Of course, this is speculation, but I present it as a suggestion for your consideration.

The other possibility is that the interstitial energy content of the universe was much higher following creation and that, as the universe expanded, the energy content also decreased per unit volume but not as rapidly as the mass density decreased. Therefore, today the overall mass density is estimated in the visible universe, and the measured residual energy density is as described previously. The current secular estimates of mass and energy do not exclude a larger universe than is currently visible. Of course, a larger universe and increased energy density following creation are not necessarily mutually exclusive, and God may have designed the residual energy density of the universe to be enough to allow rapid initial expansion up to the peak that is observed in the Hubble curve. But if the residual energy density was as measured today God knew that the universe had to expand to counteract the effects of gravity on the smaller universe, as the Bible relates, or the universe would collapse. Therefore, the conclusion is that God, omnipotent and benevolent, caused the universe to expand as the Bible tells us.

One conclusion that can be drawn in the biblical model is that there is no need to use the Hubble parameter to calculate the age of the universe. Our primary assumption for the calculations and plots presented is that ours is a young universe.

"But God made the earth by his power; he founded the world by his wisdom and stretched out the heavens by his understanding." (Jeremiah 10:12 NIV)

"I am the Lord, who has made all things, who alone stretched out the heavens who spread out the earth by myself." (Isaiah 44:24 NIV)

CHAPTER 5

Expansion of the Universe

Unless otherwise noted, all curve fittings, formulas, graphs, and plots were performed using Scientific WP.

Scale Factor

The scale factor is a parameter that characterizes the property of the expansion of the universe, reflecting an increase in distance between two points (e.g., two stars) with the passage of time. Therefore, the scale factor is a function of time and can be applied to the entire universe at any given moment. By convention (current secular usage) the scale factor is equal to 1 at the present time.[1] The scale factor is usually denoted by the lowercase letter (a) and its relation to time denoted by a(t), so the scale factor at the present time is $a(t_0) = 1$.[2] The designation t_0 refers to the reference time, which is the current epoch by secular convention (e.g., AD 2000). However, for the purposes of the biblical model, t_0 is six thousand years after creation, with t being 0 at the beginning of creation week, and t_0 corresponding to AD 2000. Therefore, the scale factor at year AM 6000 will, by definition, still be equal to 1 in the simple biblical model of creation.

The Hubble constant is also associated with the scale factor of the universe. In fact, the Hubble parameter is defined as the first derivative of the scale factor with respect to time, divided by the scale factor. Mathematically, then, the Hubble parameter (H) is:

$$H \equiv \dot{a}(t) / a(t),$$

where á represents the time derivative of the scale factor.

A different technique was used in the curve-fitting routine demonstrated in this chapter. A full-sized graph with multiple plots demonstrates a scale of "average distance between galaxies" on the Y-axis and "billions of years from now" on the X-axis. However, since the biblical model requires an early universe, the current time ($a(t_0)$) was plotted as six thousand years after creation. I superimposed the chart on graph paper and reconstructed the curve that uses $\Omega_M = 0.3$ and $\Omega_\Lambda = 0.7$. Ω represents the observed value of density parameters in the universe, while Ω_M denotes the mass density present, and Ω_Λ represents the energy density. This curve represents an initially accelerating universe, followed by deceleration and then resumed acceleration. Adding these density parameters gives 1, the total mass/ energy in the universe. There are other combinations—both can equal zero, for example—but the present context is reflective of the parameters being $0 < \Omega_M < 1$ and $\Omega_\Lambda = 1 - \Omega_M$. Figure 1 shows curves that reflect these combinations, with the corresponding formulas provided in the reference.[3]

The approach presented in this chapter can give all of the curves in Figure 1, depending on the parameters used, but for the biblical model the analysis is limited to the best theoretical plot shown, based on the currently accepted distribution of energy/matter by the secular community.[4]

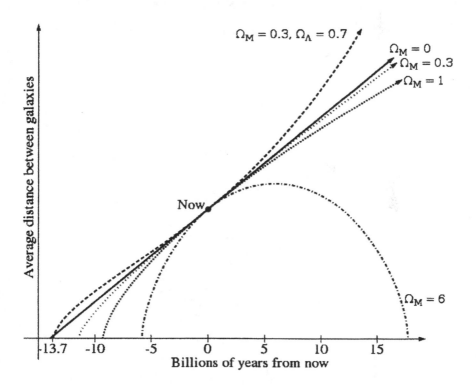

Figure 1. A composite graph of various plots representing the fate of the universe.

After I transferred the upper curve in Figure 1 to graph paper, I obtained some approximate values from the transferred graph for the corresponding scale factor in relationship to the time since creation and correlated six thousand years on the time scale with the value of a(t) = 1. These values are shown in Table 1.

The result of the curve-fitting routine using what is represented to be an exact solution to the Friedmann equations [5] is shown in a formula that represents the sinusoidal plot that results from the values shown above for Ω_M and Ω_Λ:

$$a(t) = (\Omega_M / \Omega_\Lambda \; \sinh^2 (3/2 \sqrt{\Omega_\Lambda} \; H_0 t))^{1/3}$$

However, after values for the parameters indicated were added, a prominent square wave appearance resulted, as shown in Figure 2.

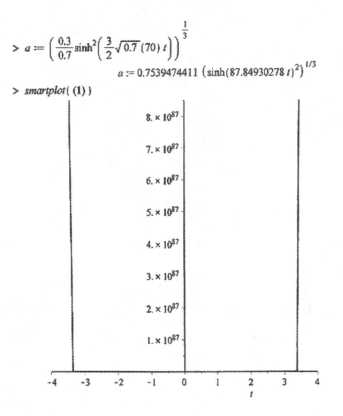

$$> a := \left(\frac{0.3}{0.7} \sinh^2 \left(\frac{3}{2} \sqrt{0.7} \, (70) \, t \right) \right)^{\frac{1}{3}}$$

$$a := 0.7539474411 \left(\sinh(87.84930278 \, t)^2 \right)^{1/3}$$

$> smartplot((1))$

Figure 2: Plot of the Friedmann equation showing the prominent square wave appearance. (Plot and calculation were performed using Maplesoft™.)

The plot in Figure 2 does not have the appearance of the sinusoidal plot shown as the top graph in Figure 1.

t	a
0.1	0.001
200	0.1
1406	0.3
2812	0.5
6000	1
8625	1.5
10913	2
12375	2.5
13688	3

Table 1: In this database the time (t) is in years, and (a) is the scale factor.

I used the Scientific WP program to obtain a polynomial fit, with a cubic equation appearing to be the best fit to the data.

The calculated polynomial fit for this database is:

$$a(t) = 1.004 \times 10^{-12} t^3 - 1.2645 \times 10^{-8} t^2 + 2.0179 \times 10^{-4} t + 2.9032 \times 10^{-2}$$

And the roots are: $6368.6 + 12738.i$, $6368.6 - 12738.i$, and -142.57

The plot of this polynomial equation is shown in Figure 3. Only a few data points are necessary to illustrate the concept and the process described in this section.

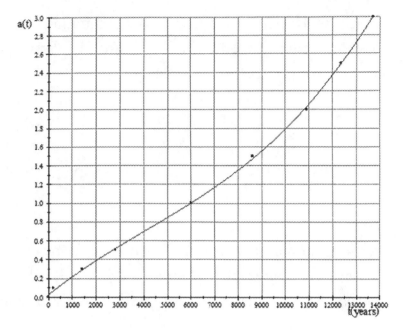

Figure 3: Plot of the values presented in Table 1.

Figure 3 shows that there is a relatively good curve fit for the database values. Continuing on, the first derivative is calculated to be:

$$\dot{a}(t) = 3.012 \times 10^{-12}t^2 - 2.529 \times 10^{-8}t + 2.0179 \times 10^{-4}$$

Calculating the Hubble Parameter

Since, by definition, the Hubble parameter is the first derivative of a(t) divided by a(t)—that is, $H \equiv \dot{a}(t) / a(t)$—there is a check on the procedure used and the formulas calculated. The dot over the (a) indicates the first derivative with respect to time.

Therefore the Hubble parameter can be calculated from these two formulas, a(t) and ȧ(t). The result of substituting the only real root of the primary formula is:

$$H = (3.012 \times 10^{-12} (-142.57)^2 - 2.529 \times 10^{-8} (-142.57)$$
$$+ 2.0179 \times 10^{-4}) \div (1.004 \times 10^{-12} (-142.57)^3 - (1.2645 \times 10^{-8} (-142.57)^2 + 2.0179 \times 10^{-4} (-142.57) + 2.9032 \times 10^{-2}) = 71.704$$

This result is the same value that is measured in the current era for the Hubble parameter. Therefore, this result validates the approach I have taken in this section of the biblical model.

z Values

The z value is another parameter that astronomers and cosmologists use in conjunction with the Hubble parameter and scale factor. The z value is used to describe the redshift of a radiation source that is visible in the universe. Redshift is defined as a proportional increase in wavelength that is observed when spectral lines that are identified in an optical spectrum from a light source in the universe are displaced toward the red or infrared portion of the electromagnetic spectrum. This change in wavelength from laboratory reference spectral lines (for a given element) is usually referred to as redshift.[6]

Redshift is interpreted as the source of the spectrum moving away from the observer. Blueshift is also possible if a visible radiation source in the universe is moving toward the observer.

Vestal Slipher saw this phenomenon in 1912 in studying what were known at the time as spiral nebulae. Since then, this observation has been used as confirmation of the Big Bang Theory and the expanding universe. The biblical model agrees with the evidence that indicates that the universe is expanding but rejects wholeheartedly the Big Bang Theory.

The redshift is calculated as a ratio between the wavelengths, or frequency, of light that is seen in the laboratory compared to that what is observed from a distant object. Mathematically, this ratio is expressed as:

$$z = (\lambda_{obs} - \lambda_{emit}) / \lambda_{emit}$$

This basic formula is used in cosmology to calculate the cosmological red shift, which is felt to be the most prominent cause for redshift observed from distant light sources in the universe. The formula used to correlate the redshift values to the scale factor is:

$$a_{then} = a_{now} / (1+z)$$

The value for a_{now} is, by secular consensus, equal to 1, so a redshift that determined to be 9, for example, would be equal to 1 divided by 10, or 0.1. Other causes for redshift are the relativistic Doppler effect and gravitational redshift.[7] All three factors may be causes for a measured redshift in the particular spectrum, but the metric expansion of space that produces the cosmological redshift is the most prominent, especially when one is observing distant light sources.

Table 2 lists a number of light sources with their astronomical designations, the z values that have been assigned to them, and their calculated scale factor numbers.

Source Designation	Assigned z Value	Calculated (a) Value
TN J0924-2201	5.2	0.1923
SDSS J1148+5251	6.42	0.1588
CFHQSJ2329-0301	6.43	0.1555
IOK-1	6.96	0.1437
A1689-ZD1	7.6	0.1316
GRB 090423	8.2	0.1220
UDFy-38135539	8.6	0.1163
UDFj-39546284	10 (tentative)	0.0909

Table 2. The assigned identifier of the source radiation with the designated z values and the calculated scale factor calculated from the z number.[8, 9]

In order to plot these light sources on a graph, we must calculate the time values for each of the sources. For example, from the previously derived formula for a(t):

$$0.1923 = 1.004 \times 10^{-12} t^3 - 1.2645 \times 10^{-8} t^2 + 2.0179 \times 10^{-4} t + 2.9032 \times 10^{-2}$$

The solutions are: $5871.6 + 12512.i$, $5871.6 - 12512.i$, and 851.33

The real result (851.33) is the first point in the table, for the a(t) value of 0.1923. Doing this for each light source gives the values shown in Table 3.

t	a
851.33	0.1923
669.6	0.1588
651.9	0.1555
588.89	0.1437
524.76	0.1316
474.22	0.1220
444.35	0.1163
312.52	0.0909

Table 3: The (a) values vs. time (t) values for the representative light sources shown in Table 2.

These values are plotted on a composite graph in Figure 4. There appears to be a relatively good correlation between the curve plotted from the data used and the formula calculated from them.

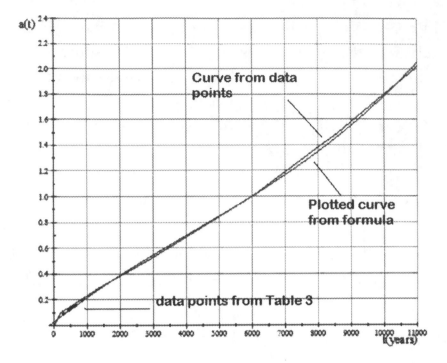

Figure 4: Composite graph with the plots of the original database, the calculated plot from the fitted formula, and the light source data.

Another calculation can be made using these values. The secular community gives a z value for decoupling as 1091.89. However, the biblical model gives a decoupling value of:

$$a = 1.004 \times 10^{-12}(0)^3 - 1.2645 \times 10^{-8}(0)^2 + 2.0179 \times 10^{-4}(0) + 2.9032 \times 10^{-2} = 2.9032 \times 10^{-2}$$

Therefore, calculations based on our biblical model of the universe gives (a) at the time of decoupling (t (0)) as 0.0290.

Therefore, z (redshift) of decoupling in the biblical model is:

$$z = (1 \div (2.9032 \times 10^{-2})) - 1 = 33.445$$

Since our graph is in years, a zero value can be used for the time of decoupling since any decoupling is likely to have occurred during the first day of creation, as seen in the Bible: "God saw that the light was good, and he separated the light from the darkness" (Genesis 1:4 NIV). A prediction from this calculation indicates that no source of light with a z value greater than 33.445 is observable.

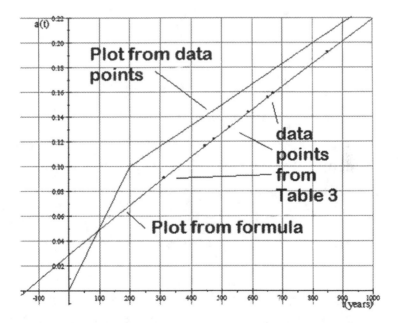

Figure 5: A coned-down view of the early created universe, showing a plot from the fitted curve with a representative sample of radiation sources and their calculated (a) values

plotted on the graph. The second line connects the lower data points used for the curve fit, shown in the previous section, Table 1.

One additional observation about the plots presented in the data points represented by and on the plots shown in this section is that the representative plot from the derived formula intersects the (a) axis but does not intersect at $(0, 0)$ as one might expect if the universe started as a singularity. However, the created universe was created with a finite size, so the curves plotted represent an already existing scale factor for the created universe in the immediate seconds and hours following God's act of creation. In other words, God created the universe with a finite size to begin with.

Therefore, the application of the scale factor (a) to the universe as a whole works well for an early created universe, as opposed to the big bang model. The scale factor plot is another demonstration that the early universe model is as scientifically valid as an ancient universe model.

Metric Expansion of Space

In the secular literature, the metric expansion of space is defined as the average distance between distant objects, usually increasing, over time. The relative expansion of galaxies, stars, and so on appears to be a prominent feature of the secular Big Bang cosmology. Metric expansion is not

viewed to be outward expansion of the universe itself; "…
the question of what the universe is expanding into is one
which does not require an answer according to the theories
which describe the expansion; …There is no reason to
believe there is anything 'outside' of the expanding universe
into which the universe expands." [10]

Although special relativity precludes material objects from
moving faster than the speed of light, there is no theoretical
restraint on space itself, which may expand faster than the
speed of light. According to the ΛCDM (Lambda Cold Dark
Matter) model, the cosmological constant (Λ) will dominate
in the future.[11] Our simple biblical cosmological model
conforms to this concept as well—that is that the interstitial
energy content will dominate in the future—but there is no
such thing as cold dark matter.

Contrary to the secular review of the metric expansion of
space, the biblical model considers that the metric expansion
of space is outward and constructs the expansion curve
accordingly. The simple biblical model of the universe has
no difficulty answering the question asked by the article,
"What space is the universe expanding into?" The answer
is that the universe is expanding into the Third Heaven,
as mentioned in 2 Cor. 12:2. In order to show this concept
graphically a segment of expanding universe is illustrated
in Figure 6.

The diagram in Figure 6 expresses the point of creation, with God creating all of the energy necessary in the universe: "And God said, 'Let there be light,' and there was light" (Genesis 1:3 NIV). The derivation of a metric expansion formula is the next step.

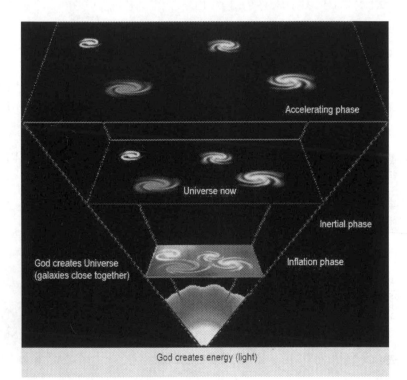

Figure 6: Illustration of the overall concept of the creation and expansion of the universe.

Database

The database for the metric expansion formula was obtained much like that in the previous section, but in taking the approximate measurements from the plot shown in Figure 1, I obtained radii in kilometers, with time along the X-axis in seconds instead of having a scale factor on the Y-axis. Two points were fixed on this curve: at 0 seconds the universe was plotted with a radius of six thousand light years (5.672×10^{16} km), and the radius for the year 2000 was plotted at 4.399×10^{23} km with a time of 1.8662×10^{11} seconds for six thousand years (see Figure 1). The extracted database is given as Table 4.

t (sec)	r (Km)
0	5.672×10^{16}
7.775×10^{9}	4.5×10^{22}
1.555×10^{10}	7.91×10^{22}
2.3325×10^{10}	1.5×10^{23}
3.11×10^{10}	1.9×10^{23}
4.665×10^{10}	2.6×10^{23}
6.22×10^{10}	3.1×10^{23}
7.775×10^{10}	3.4×10^{23}
9.33×10^{10}	3.6×10^{23}
1.244×10^{11}	3.8×10^{23}
1.555×10^{11}	4.1×10^{23}
1.866×10^{11}	4.399×10^{23}
2.177×10^{11}	5.8×10^{23}
2.488×10^{11}	1×10^{24}
2.8×10^{11}	1.8×10^{24}

Table 4. Database for the metric expansion plot.

The initial, raw formula is:

$$r = .3.2549 \times 10^{-10} t^3 - 110.57\, t^2 + 1.1866 \times 10^{13}\, t - 5.5377 \times 10^{22}$$

However, a preliminary modification must be made, as the radius at creation (time 0) is, according to our model, 5.672×10^{16} km. If we set $t = 0$, then $r =$ the radius at that time, and the formula *must* be adjusted to reflect this. I also adjusted the formula to improve its conformity with the data points selected. Thus, we get a relatively simple, modified formula:

$$r = 2.2 \times 10^{-10} t^3 - 76t^2 + 0.9 \times 10^{13}\, t + 5.672 \times 10^{16}$$

And the roots are:

$1.7273 \times 10^{11} - 1.0523 \times 10^{11}\, i,\ 1.7273 \times 10^{11} + 1.0523 \times 10^{11}\, i$, and -6302.2

The plot of our modified formula is shown in Figure 7. The initial portions of the curve conform well to the data points that were obtained from the graph in Figure 1. The later portion of the curve deviates somewhat from those listed in the database, suggesting a somewhat slower, although still accelerating, expansion.

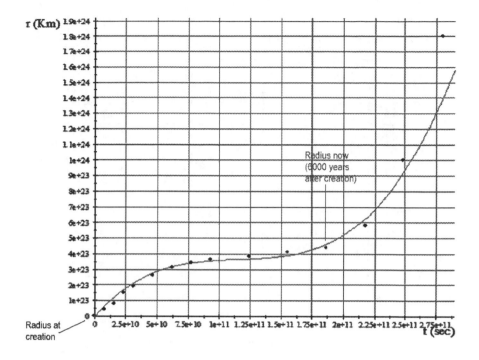

Figure 7: Plot of the expansion of the universe from creation

One of the goals of this portion of the evaluation of the metric expansion of space is to evaluate the possibility of a large acceleration immediately following creation. There may have been some acceleration initially, but this acceleration appears to have been minimal. Of course, the initial portion of the curve is compatible with the inflationary period, followed by an inertial period, resulting in a relative plateau at the present time. Referring to the Hubble curve, this view conforms to the minimum portion of the curve at about six thousand years after creation (AD 2000).

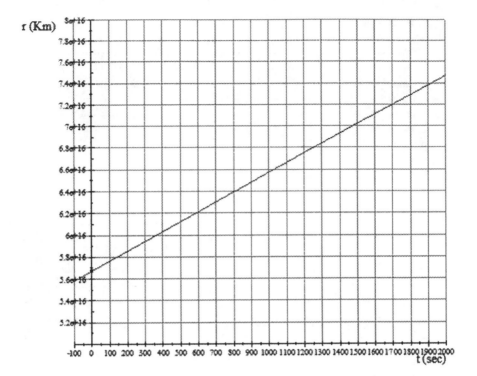

Figure 8. Coned-down view of the beginning of the modified curve, showing the initial radius of the universe at 5.672×10^{16} km.

Because the created universe began with a definite radius and because we are plotting the time coordinates in seconds, the calculation and plots demand a large number for the time, and the radius in kilometers demands a large number for the r value. The first derivative of this formula is:

$$r' = 6.6 \times 10^{-10}\, t^2 - 152\, t + 9.0 \times 10^{12}$$

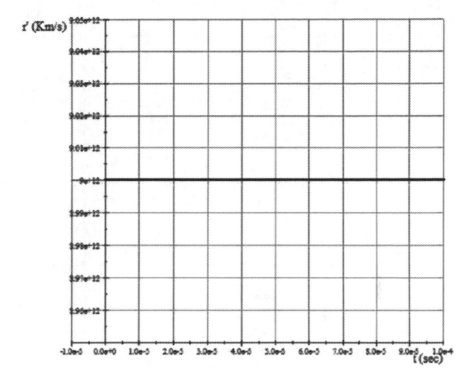

Figure 9. A focal view of the first derivative plot following time 0.

The slope should represent the acceleration (km/s vs. s). The curve is flat; that is, no detectible acceleration appears in the initial fraction of a second after creation. According to the biblical model, there is no evidence of a rapid expansion at the time of the beginning of the universe, that is, at creation.

The second derivative of our formula is:

$$r'' = 1.32 \times 10^{-9}\,t - 152$$

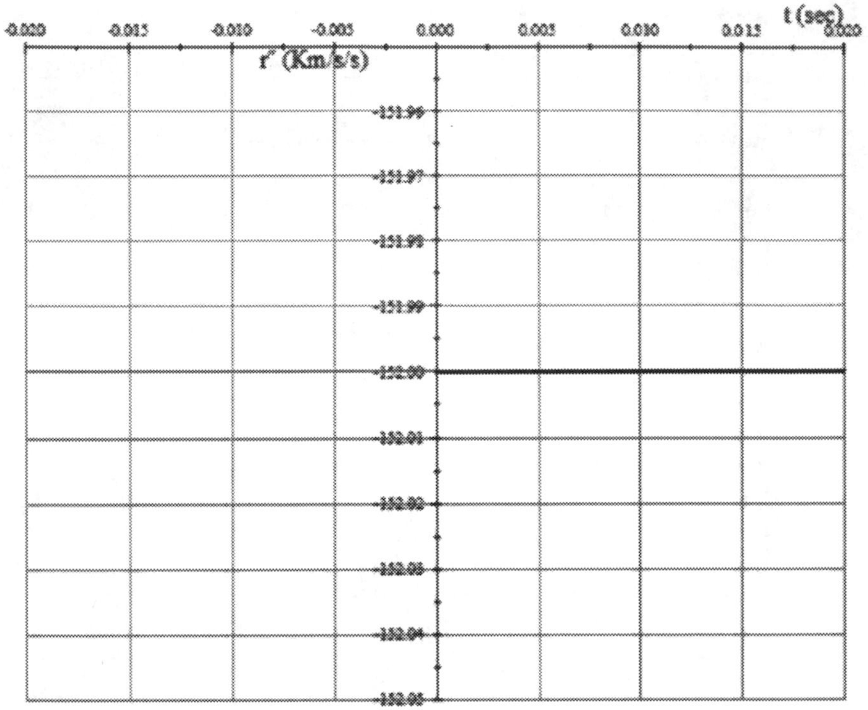

Figure 10: Second derivative plot.

Referring to the section on the Hubble curve, the acceleration at the beginning of the universe, as calculated from the previous curve, was 3.5411×10^{-7} km/s/s. That is low acceleration at best. The second derivative plot shows a flat curve, with a negative value of 152 km/s/s, suggesting that there would have been at least a theoretical negative acceleration (that is a collapse or contraction) immediately after creation because of the mass of created matter in relation to the radius of the universe at creation. However, God, in His wisdom, then caused the universe to expand (as the Bible tells us) in an orderly and essentially constant fashion in order to prevent it from collapsing on itself.

Conclusions

This chapter shows that the approach used in cosmology by secular science is applicable to a young universe model because the concept of the scale factor can be applied to such a universe and using the formulas derived by computer analysis satisfies the requirement for the definition of the Hubble parameter.

In addition to constructing a curve that demonstrates the scale factor of the universe, I also showed a plot that correlates a similar curve that relates the actual dimensions of the universe to a biblical six-thousand-year timescale. In deriving the radius vs time formula; I assumed that the universe has a minimal radius of six thousand light years. Therefore, the endpoints of the first portion of the plotted curve are the minimum radius of the universe and the estimated radius of the universe at the year 2000. The resulting curve is similar in appearance to the scale factor curve, which is not surprising, as both are based on the secular assumption that $\Omega_M = 0.3$ and $\Omega_\Lambda = 0.7$ and the plot shown in Figure 1.

This chapter also demonstrated, in conjunction with the application of the concept of the scale factor to a young universe, that the secular formulation of the redshift, or z parameter, can be applied to a young universe. The computed curves intersect the scale factor axis above zero, which confirms that the universe was created at a finite size by an omnipotent God.

Several representative samples of light sources in the universe are plotted on the metric expansion of space curve. The curve also demonstrates that there is further space, more distant than the most recent distant light emitting object discovered, which has a tentative z value of 10. The conclusion is that the appearance of the curve to the left of this z value correlates with an earlier discussion of the possibility that the universe is likely larger than that visible at the present time—possibly as much as a billion times larger.

The formulas derived in this simple biblical model of cosmology can be seen as substitutes for the more complex formulas that secular science has used to describe the early universe and the current universe. Therefore, the biblical model has simpler mathematics than the current secular models.

It is evident from all of these curves that there was an initial expansion phase of the universe, followed by an inertial phase, with an essentially quiescent phase at the present time. However the prediction of all of these curves indicates that the universe will continue to expand at an ever-increasing rate, as the interstitial energy of the universe continues to be replaced and exceeds the gravitational attraction of the mass/energy present. Therefore, the prediction of the curves shown in this simple biblical model of cosmology is that the universe will continue to accelerate in size and velocity unless God Almighty intervenes. This prediction suggests that the most distant galaxies may not be visible in the relatively near future, and, as the model predicts, no visible light source with a z value greater than approximately 30 will be detected. Therefore, it remains to be seen whether the James Webb space telescope will be able to reveal significantly more distant galaxies than those currently visible. For now, a young universe and a young Earth are shown to be compatible with the parameters and astronomical measurements made by secular cosmologists.

"He then brought them out and asked, 'Sirs, what must I do to be saved?' They replied, 'Believe in the Lord Jesus, and you will be saved.'" (Acts 16:30–31 NIV)

Notes

Chapter 1

1. *NOAA Ocean Explorer*: Observations on the Gulf Stream: http:// oceanexplorer.noaa.gov/library/reading/gulf/gulf.html.
2. Matthew Fontaine Maury: http://en.wikipedia.org/wiki/Matthew_ Fontaine_Maury.
3. Comet. *Wikipedia*, the Free Encyclopedia. http://en.wikipedia.org/ wiki/Comet.
4. *Digital Journal*: http://www.digitaljournal.com/article/309433.
5. Hawking, Stephen. (1996). *A Brief History of Time*. Bantam Books: New York: 49.
6. DiVenere, Vic. (2011). The Origin of the Universe and the Earth. Columbia University Summer Session 2011. http://www.columbia. edu/~ vjdl/origins.htm.
7. Big Bang Theory: The Premise. *All about Science*. http://big-bang-theory.com/.
8. Big Bang. *Wikipedia*, the Free Encyclopedia. http://en/ Wikipediaorg/wiki/Big Bang.
9. Recombination (cosmology). *Wikipedia*, the Free Encyclopedia. http://en.wikipedia.org/wiki/Recombination (cosmology).
10. Humphries, Russell._Our Galaxy Is the Center of the Universe. http://creation.com/our-galaxy-is-the-center-of-the-universe-quantized-redshifts-show.

Chapter 2

1. Jason, Eric, and Macmillan, Steve. 2005. *Astronomy Today.* Upper Saddle River, NJ: Pearson Prentice Hall, 695.

2. Observable Universe. (2010). *Wikipedia*, the Free Encyclopedia. http://en.wikipedia.org/wiki/Mass of the observable universe.

3. Powell, James R. 2008. Unification of Fundamental Forces at High Radiation Temperature in the Creator: The Consuming Fire. *CRSQ* 34:18–23.

4. Tang, K. T. 2007. Mathematical Models for Engineers and Scientists 3. Berlin: Springer-Verlag, 311.

5. Tang, K. T. 2007. Mathematical Models for Engineers and Scientists 3. Berlin: Springer-Verlag, 278.

6. Bates, Stephen C. 2002. Compilation of the Engineering Properties of Solid Hydrogen. http://www.tvu.com/PEngPropsSH2Web.htm

7. Akridge, Russell, Barnes, Thomas, and Slusher, Harold S. 1981. A Recent Creation Explanation of the 3° K Background Black Body Radiation. *CRSQ.* 159–162.

Chapter 3

1. Carroll, S. Dark Matter, Dark Energy: The Dark Side of the Universe. 2007. Chantilly, VA: The Teaching Company.

2. Urry, Meg. 2008. The Mysteries of Dark Energy. Yale University. http://castroller.com/podcasts/yalescience/O.

3. Cosmological Constant. 2010. http://en. Wikipedia.org/wiki/cosmological constant

4. Perlmutter, S. et al. 1990. Measurements of Φ and $\otimes$ from 42 High-Red Shift Supernovae. *The Astrophysical Journal* 517:565–586.

5. Carroll, S., 2007. Dark Matter, Dark Energy: The Dark Side of the Universe. Chantilly, VA: The Teaching Company, 66.

6. Carroll, S., 2007. Dark Matter, Dark Energy: The Dark Side of the Universe. Chantilly, VA: The Teaching Company, 68.

7. Cheng, C. 2000. Density of the Universe. *The Physics Factbook*. Wikipedia, http://hypertextook.com/facts/2000/ChristinaCheng.shtml

8. Carmelli, Moshe. Relativity: Modern Large Scale Space-time Structure of the Cosmos. Singapore: World Scientific Publishing Company Ltd., 64.

9. Carmelli, Moshe. Relativity: Modern Large Scale Space-time Structure of the Cosmos. Singapore: World Scientific Publishing Company Ltd., 359.

10. Weiss, M. and Gupta, A. The Milky Way's Hot Gas Halo. http://www. nasa.gov/mission_pages/chandra/multimedia/hot_gas_halo.html

11. Sanders, J. et al. Clues to the Growth of the Colossus in Coma. http://www.nasa.gov/mission_pages/chandra/multimedia/-cluster-growth.html

12. Hartnett, John. 2007. Starlight, Time and the New Physics. Australia: Creation Book Publishers, 122.

13. Carroll, Sean M. Spacetime and Geometry: An Introduction to General Relativity. 2004. San Francisco: Addison Wesley Publishers, 172.

14. Carroll, Sean M. Spacetime and Geometry: An Introduction to General Relativity. 2004. San Francisco: Addison Wesley Publishers, 174.

15. Chaisson, E. and McMillan, S. 2005. *Astronomy Today*, 5th Ed. Fahlgren, E., Ed. Upper Saddle River, NJ: Pearson Prentice Hall, 402–597.

16. Savage, B. D. 1987. The Properties of the Gaseous Galactic Corona. No. 6.The Origin of Galactic Halo Gas. <http://nedwww. ipac.Caltech.edu/level5/ Savage/Savage6.html>.

17. Pogge, R., 2006. Lecture 27: Spirals & Ellipticals & Irregulars (oh my!), *Astronomy 162* http://www.astronomy.ohiostate.edu/~pogge/ Ast162/Unit4/types.html. Accessed 2/21/2011.

18. Darling, D. Elliptical Galaxy. *Internet Encyclopedia of Science.* <http://www.daviddarling.info/lowercase encyclopedia/E/ elliptical.html. >

19. Barstow, M.A. 2005. Elliptical Galaxies. http/www.star.le.ac.uk/ edu/edu/Elliptical.shtml

20. Pogge, R. 2006. Lecture 27: Spirals & Ellipticals & Irregulars (oh my!). *Astronomy 162* http://www.astronomy.ohiostate.edu/~pogge/ Ast162/ Unit4/types.html.

21. Korista, K. T. "Important Properties of Galaxies". http:// homepages.wmich.edu/~korista/galaxy-why.html.

22. Mackie, G. 1999. To See the Universe in a Grain of Toranaki Sand. http://astronomy.swin.edu.au/~gmackie/billions.html

23. Murray, T., 1999. "Number of Galaxies in the Universe". Elert, Glenn (Ed.).http://hypertextbook.com/facts/1999/TopazMurray. shtml

24. Chaisson, E. and McMillan, S. 2005. *Astronomy Today,* 5th Ed. Fahlgren, E., Ed. Upper Saddle River, NJ: Pearson Prentice Hall, 402–597.

25. ESA. 2004. How Many Stars Are There in the Universe? *ESA Space Science.* http://www.esa.int/esaSC/SEM75BSIVED_index_O.html.

26. Galaxy Groups and Clusters. *New World Encyclopedia, 2009.* http://www.newworldencyclopedia.org/entry/Galaxy-groups-and-clusters

27. Keel, B. 2009. The Intergalactic Medium in Galaxies and the Universe. http://www.astr.ua.edu/keel/galaxies/igm.html

28. Supercluster. 2011. *Economic Expert*. http://www.economicexpert.com/a/Supercluster.htm

29. Paerels, F. et al. 2010. X-ray Spectroscopy of the Warm-Hot Intergalactic Medium. White Paper Submitted to the Astro 2010 Decadal Survey of Astronomy and Astrophysics.

30. Quasar. 2011. Wikipedia, the Free Encyclopedia. http://en.wikipedia.org/wiki/Quasar.

31. Observable Universe. 2011. Wikipedia, the Free Encyclopedia. http://en.wikipedia.org/wiki/Observable_universe

32. Carroll, Sean M. The Cosmological Constant. http://nedwww.ipac.caltech.edu/level5/Carroll2/Carroll1_3.html

33. *Ibid.*

34. Interstellar Medium. 2009. Wikipedia, the Free Encyclopedia. http://en.wikipedia.org/wiki/Interstellar

35. Cheng, C. 2000. Density of the Universe. *The Physics Factbook*. G. Elert, Ed. Wikipedia, the Free Encyclopedia. http://hypertextook.com/facts/2000/ChristinaCheng.shtml

36. Nave, R. Division of Energy between Photons and Massive Particles. http://hyperphysics.phy-ast.gsu.edu/hbase/Astro/expand.html

37. Guth, Allen H. 1997. The Inflationary Universe. Perseus Books, 186. http://www.perseuspublishing.com

38. Cheng, C. 2000. Density of the Universe. *The Physics Factbook*. G. Elert, Ed. Wikipedia, http://hypertextook.com/facts/2000/ChristinaCheng.shtml

39. Einstein Field Equations. Wikipedia, the Free Encyclopedia. http://en.wikipedia.org/wiki/Einstein%27s_equations

40. Static Universe. Wikipedia, the Free Encyclopedia. http://en.wikipedia.org/wiki/ Static_Universe

41. Einstein Field Equations. Wikipedia, the Free Encyclopedia. http://en.wikipedia.org/ wiki/Einstein%27s_equations

42. Hartnett, John. 2005. Dark matter and a cosmological constant in a creationist cosmology. *Journal of Creation*, 19(1):82–87.

43. Markey, Sean. October 8, 2003. Universe Is Finite, "Soccer Ball"-Shaped, Study Hints. *National Geographic News*. http://news.nationalgeographic.com/news/2003/10/1008   031008 finiteuniverse.html

44. Wilkinson Microwave Anisotropy Probe. Wikipedia, the Free Encyclopedia. http://en.wikipedia.org/wiki/WMAP

45. General Relativity: Why does pressure act as a source for the gravitational field? *Physics*. http://physics.stackexchange.com/questions/3688/why-does-pressure-act-as-a-source-for-the-gravitational-field?

46. Humphries, Russ. New time dilatation helps creation cosmology. http://creation.com/new-time-dilitation-helps-creation-cosmology

47. Absolute zero. Wikipedia, the Free Encyclopedia. http://en.wikipedia.org/wiki/Absolute_zero

48. Carroll, Sean M. and Press, William H. 1992. The Cosmological Constant. *Annu._Rev. Astron. Astrophys.* 30:499–542.

49. Carroll, Sean M. 2004. Spacetime and Geometry: An Introduction to General Relativity. San Francisco: Addison Wesley, 35.

50. Wall, Mike. January 26, 2011. Oldest galaxy: Hubble telescope detects furthest, oldest galaxy yet. *The Christian Science Monitor*. http://www.csmonitor.com/layout/set/r14/Science/2011/0126/Oldest-galaxy-Hubble-telescope-detects-furthestoldest-galaxy-yet

51. Hwang, J. and Noh, H. 2006. Why Newtonian gravity is reliable in large-scale cosmological simulations. *Mon. Not. R. Astron. Soc.* 367, 1515–1520.

52. Bunn, Ted. Why does pressure act as a source for the gravitational field? http://physics.stackexchange.com/questions/3688/why-does-pressure-act-as-a-source-for-the-gravitational-field?

53. Wright, Ned. 1998. Vacuum Energy Density, or How Can Nothing Weigh Something? http://www.astro.ucla.edu/~wright/cosmoconstant.html.

54. Shell Theorem. 2011. Wikipedia, the Free Encyclopedia. http://en.wikipedia.org/wiki/Shelltheorem

55. Nave, R. Pressure. http://hyperphysics.phy-astr.gsu.edu/hbase/press.html.

56. Humphries, Russ. New time dilatation helps creation cosmology. http://creation.com/new-time-dilitation-helps-creation-cosmology

57. Riess, Adam G. and Filippenko, Alexi V.1998. Observational Evidence from Supernova for an Accelerating Universe and a Cosmological Constant. *The Astronomical Journal* 116:1009–1038.

Chapter 4

1. Hubble's Law. Wikipedia, the Free Encyclopedia. http://en.wikipedia.org.wiki/Hubbleparameter

2. Livio, Mario. The World according to the Hubble Space Telescope: The Hubble constant. http://ned.ipac.caltech.Edu/level5/March03/Livio/Livio7.html

3. Cosmological Parameters. http://burro.cwru.edu/Academics/Astr328/Notes/Expansion/parameters.html.

4. Wright, Ned. Frequently Ask Questions in Cosmology. http://www.astro.ucla.edu/~wright/cosmology_faq.html

5. Huchra, John P. The Hubble Constant. https://www.cfa.harvard.edu/~dfabricant/huchra/hubble/h1920.jpg

6. Huchra, John P. The Hubble Constant. https://www.cfa.harvard.edu/~defabricant/huchra/hubble/h1970.jpg

7. Huchra, John. The Hubble Constant. https://www.cfa.harvard.edu/~defabricant/huchra/hubble/

Chapter 5

1. Metric Expansion of Space. Wikipedia, the Free Encyclopedia. http://en.wikipedia.org/wiki/Metricexpansionofspace

2. Scale factor (cosmology). Wikipedia, the Free Encyclopedia. http://en.wikipedia.org/wiki/Scale_factor_(cosmology)

3. File: Friedman universes.svg. Wikipedia, the Free Encyclopedia. http://en.wikipedia.org/wiki/File:Friedman universes.svg

4. Carroll, Sean M. 2004. Spacetime and Geometry: An Introduction to General Relativity. San Francisco: Addison Wesley, 343.

5. File: Friedman universes.svg. Wikipedia, the Free Encyclopedia. http://en.wikipedia.org/wiki/File:Friedmanuniverses.svg

6. Redshift. Wikipedia, the Free Encyclopedia. http://en.wikipedia.org/wiki/Redshift

7. *Ibid.*

8. *Ibid.*

9. Villard, Ray, Illingworth, G., and Bouwens, R. NASA's Hubble Finds Most Distant Galaxy Candidate Ever Seen in Universe. http://hubblesite.org/newscenter/archive/releases/2011/05/full/

10. Metric expansion of space. Wikipedia, the Free Encyclopedia. http://en.wikipedia.org/wiki/Metricexpansionofspace

11. Ibid.

"I am not ashamed of the gospel, because it is the power of God for the salvation of everyone who believes: first for the Jew, then for the Gentile." (Rom. 1:16 NIV)